AF763220

GROWING UP AND OUT OF CRIME

Developmental norms and expectations for young people aged 18–25 have diverged from previous generations, shifting the role of maturation that prompts us to examine if and how this maturation can influence desistance from crime.

Utilizing evidence from the narratives of justice-involved emerging adults, this book details key turning points for young people trying to desist from crime. Building on evidence from researchers and theorists as well as from the author's own narrative interviews, this book offers a brief and approachable review of the extant literature, summarizing work across the fields of developmental psychology, sociology, and criminology to provide the reader with an understanding of the maturation of young people in their late teens and 20s before concluding with considerations for policy and practice building from this evidence.

Growing Up and Out of Crime is perfect for students, scholars, and academics who study young people and behavior across the life course and maturation, deviance, and desistance as well as for practitioners working on desistance or working with young people engaged in deviance.

Elias S. Nader, PhD, is an assistant professor in the Department of Sociology and Criminology at Kent State University. He is a criminologist who studies two main topic areas: the transition to adulthood among justice-involved young people and the practices, policies, and initiatives of police departments.

"Nader has produced a top-notch study that advances the field of desistance and maturation in several important ways. Written in engaging and vivid prose, Nader sheds light on not only the importance of identity transformation in emerging adulthood but also on the mechanisms through which identity shifts. The research participants' voices tell the story throughout, with Nader's deft analytic hand guiding the analysis, resulting in a vital contribution to life-course criminology and one that is sure to be a staple in classrooms for years to come."

Michael Rocque, *Bates College*

"Nader deftly integrates theory and research to address a major problem in criminology: as many of the well-known turning points supporting desistance from offending become increasingly rare, how do today's emerging adults form law-abiding identities? If marriage and employment spurred conformity for the generation after World War 2, what are the hooks for change that young people employ in the contemporary context? In answering these questions, Growing Up and Out of Crime advances the field of life course and developmental criminology and has important implications for crime policy."

Jamie J. Fader, *Temple University College of Liberal Arts*

GROWING UP AND OUT OF CRIME

Desistance, Maturation, and Emerging Adulthood

Elias S. Nader

Routledge
Taylor & Francis Group
LONDON AND NEW YORK

Designed cover image: Getty, #171248465 zodebala

First published 2024
by Routledge
4 Park Square, Milton Park, Abingdon, Oxon OX14 4RN

and by Routledge
605 Third Avenue, New York, NY 10158

Routledge is an imprint of the Taylor & Francis Group, an informa business

© 2024 Elias S. Nader

The right of Elias S. Nader to be identified as author of this work has been asserted in accordance with sections 77 and 78 of the Copyright, Designs and Patents Act 1988.

All rights reserved. No part of this book may be reprinted or reproduced or utilised in any form or by any electronic, mechanical, or other means, now known or hereafter invented, including photocopying and recording, or in any information storage or retrieval system, without permission in writing from the publishers.

Trademark notice: Product or corporate names may be trademarks or registered trademarks, and are used only for identification and explanation without intent to infringe.

British Library Cataloguing-in-Publication Data
A catalogue record for this book is available from the British Library

ISBN: 978-0-367-69858-4 (hbk)
ISBN: 978-0-367-69857-7 (pbk)
ISBN: 978-1-003-14358-1 (ebk)

DOI: 10.4324/9781003143581

Typeset in Sabon
by KnowledgeWorks Global Ltd.

This book is dedicated to all of the young people who have shared their stories with me over the years, for this project and others. Whether or not your stories were included in this text, your experiences matter and played a role in helping to shape how I understand the hurdles and barriers our social systems create for the process of growing up.

CONTENTS

INTRODUCTION

Criminologists have spent decades theorizing the developmental process and its influence on deviance and desistance. Over the years, developmental and life course criminologists have effectively utilized evidence across disciplines to help develop and refine these theories. As this subfield focuses on development through the life course, these theories leverage work in the fields of psychology, biology, and sociology to advance criminological thought. To date, most of the work within developmental and life course criminology has been focused on adolescence, youth, and the youngest of adults (ages 13–21). This focus has been driven largely in conjunction with policy, centered around the juvenile justice system and its purview over youth under the age of 18 and recent examinations of raising the age of coverage under the juvenile justice system.

In this book, I work to extend this theorization beyond juveniles into adulthood – specifically **emerging adulthood.** Within developmental psychology, emerging adulthood has become a burgeoning subfield examining the transition to adulthood in society among younger adults aged 18–29. Importantly, this subfield engages the changes in society and social dynamics for young people, largely Millennials and Generation Z, that diverge from previous generations. These include an emphasis on higher education, increased average age of marriage and parenting, and increased age of first-time home ownership (Arnett, 2000, 2016). These traditional markers of adulthood have facilitated an opportunity for Millennials, and now Generation Z, to engage in identity and role exploration that previously was indicative of adolescence.

Emerging adulthood theory argues that traditional turning points alone, such as marriage, parenthood, and employment, are not enough to facilitate

DOI: 10.4324/9781003143581-1

a transition into the identity of an adult in modern society. This theory argues that values relating to the quality of character are important markers in the transition to adulthood. These include accepting responsibility for oneself, making independent decisions, establishing a unique set of values, and becoming financially independent (Arnett, 1997, 1998, 2000; Greene et al., 1992; Scheer et al., 1996). The life phase of emerging adulthood, thus, is focused on establishing one's quality of character and values within the context of the transition into adulthood.

These qualities of character are especially important for those who face barriers in accessing traditional markers of adulthood (Arnett, 1998, 2000; Nader, 2019). When young people are restricted from, or perceive they are restricted from, certain adult roles in society, the recognition of their own development and maturation is necessary to overcome any obstructions they face. This recognition is grounded in one's perception of who they are – or their **identity** (Bamberg, 2011). Establishing one's identity is central to the developmental process, particularly for emerging adults. This life phase is one where young people are expected to engage in identity change and exploration toward a finalized adult version of themselves. Identity change and development thus offer a mechanism for emerging adults to latch onto adult roles.

This identity transformation is central to the life course and progression through it (Côté, 2002; Klimstra et al., 2010). Young people naturally engage in a process of cognitive transformation where they explore the possibilities of themselves, of the world around them, and of their role in that world (Piaget, 1951). Emerging adulthood is a time where this occurs naturally and uniquely for modern-day young people because of how this life phase is characterized by role exploration and experimentation (Arnett, 2000; Luyckx et al., 2006). Emerging adults are exploring "who they are" both psychologically and socially, trying out various roles and behaviors in an effort to settle into a finalized version of their adult self.

Identity is a key concept in the criminological literature on desistance. Identity change and development offer a path for people involved in crime to desist as they separate their past, criminal selves from their current or future law-abiding selves (Maruna, 2001; see also Giordano et al., 2002, 2007). This occurs through a series of cognitive transformations where one adapts their views of "who they are" both personally and socially. These transformations then can couple with "hooks" for change and "scaffolds" toward new social roles to allow people to latch onto accessible prosocial opportunities to embrace desistance (Giordano et al., 2002). This may be especially pivotal for those who have experienced justice-system contact or incarceration, as they may be forced to assess their own role in society and the consequences of their engagement in deviance (Paternoster & Bushway, 2009; Shover, 1996).

Criminologists have recently argued for the application of perspectives focused on the unique characteristics of modern-day young people to traditional life course theories. These works (e.g., Bersani & Doherty, 2018; Laub & Sampson, 2020; Nguyen & Loughran, 2018; Salvatore, 2017) were pivotal in my own reflection on life course theory and its consequences in empirical research on today's desisting young person. In examining how criminologists can learn from the field of emerging adulthood, I have found a lot of very convenient overlaps in foundational theories. Many developmental psychology, identity, and emerging adult scholars are thinking in line with developmental and life course criminologists. Theories under the umbrella of emerging adulthood often offer an extension of traditional developmental theories focused on adolescence, extending them to and modifying them for younger people beyond the age of 18. Throughout this book, I will present some background on the fields of emerging adulthood and developmental and life course criminology, highlighting where these two subfields can intersect and (theoretically) build upon one another.

Is This Actually "Emerging" Adulthood?

While the term *emerging* adulthood, signifying an emergence into the life stage of adulthood, works well generally for the subfields of developmental psychology, it may not be the most aptly used term within the context of criminology. As originally presented by Arnett (2000, 2016), this stage is not to be confused with *young* adulthood, as emerging adults do not view themselves as reaching adulthood. The term young adulthood comes with an implication that adulthood has been reached. Instead, the *emerging* term encompasses the dynamic quality of this stage where the transition into adulthood occurs gradually (Arnett, 2000). Young people are emerging into adulthood by exploring what being an adult means and how they can become one while balancing their personal, social, and environmental contexts.

Although the age distinctions between adolescence (up to age 18), emerging adulthood (age 18 into the late 20s), and young adulthood (late 20s to 30s) exist, they are meant to be rough markers, with every individual transitioning between these developmental stages at their own rate (Arnett, 2000, 2016). For example, emerging adulthood was originally grounded in a certain age group (18–25 years old), although in more recent theorizations Arnett and others have acknowledged that it expands beyond age 25 and into the late 20s (e.g., Arnett, 2015, 2016). Since his original theorization, Arnett has argued that emerging adulthood does not necessarily end at a specific age and that progression through this life stage is often an individualized process (Arnett, 2016). It may be that certain markers for the transition out of emerging adulthood may be met while others have not, differentiating the timeline under which a young person matures out of this life stage.

Considering the needs and barriers young people involved in the justice system often face, *emerging* adulthood may not be the ideal term to characterize their engagement with this life stage. Many variations exist across culture and class regarding what makes an adult, translating into different definitions and perspectives for individuals in what this term means and how adulthood manifests. Certainly, as with many concepts, emerging adulthood theory has received its share of critiques (e.g., Côté, 2014). In particular, DeLuca and colleagues (2016) provide a discussion of the transition to adulthood worth recognizing here as it acknowledges this disconnect in theoretically defined life stages and the lived experiences of many young people.

In their book "Coming of Age in the Other America", DeLuca and colleagues (2016) engaged in ten years of fieldwork in Baltimore with people who lived in public housing. In this research, they study low-income families and the process of growing up for young people born into circumstances of structural inequality and poverty. They find that those born into Baltimore's lowest-income families, and especially Black children in these families, had difficulties with entering the middle class as they grew up. The disadvantages they faced, including racial inequality, dangerous neighborhoods, and poorly resourced public schools, contributed to this cycle of intergenerational marginalization. Despite this, their research found that those young people "at the cusp of adulthood" were comparable to their more affluent peers in terms of hopes and aspirations for the future (DeLuca et al., 2016, p. 5). "Most were, in fact, doing exactly what young people their age are supposed to be doing – discovering what they were 'about,' cultivating dreams, and engaging in a quest to 'become somebody.'" (DeLuca et al., 2016, p. 5).

These young people had the same hopes and aspirations as peers from other socioeconomic groups, in line with what we define as culturally acceptable futures – going to college, building a career, owning a home, and having a family. Yet, in their research, Deluca and colleagues found that young people were often on an "expedited path to adulthood" as a result of their difficult economic circumstances. While much of their sample of youth did not become involved in delinquency, they often ended up working lower-wage, unstable jobs, relegating them to remain in their same socioeconomic class even if their ambitions were aimed elsewhere. Thus, they ended up in a cycle of performing this type of *expedited* adulthood, adjusting their emergence into this life stage, and not affording them the luxuries of limitless or unconditional self-exploration and experimentation indicative of their *emerging* adult peers in higher socioeconomic groups.

Young people in this expedited path to adulthood, however, still yearn to emerge into a different type of adulthood. Here, this takes the form of an **identity project**, which serves as a "virtual bridge between challenging present circumstances and an uncertain, but hoped-for, future" (DeLuca et al., 2016, p. 9). These identity projects were often related to school, career, or specific interests, such as artistic endeavors (e.g., writing poetry, writing music). Identity projects provided a blueprint for young people to engage in new activities and keep them away from delinquency or risky behaviors. The projects allowed the young people to distance themselves from relationships (e.g., family, neighborhoods) that did not match their aspirations and instead cling to other relationships or contexts to support them (e.g., teachers).

As Chapter 1 will outline, those on the expedited path exhibit many of the characteristics theorized of emerging adults. They are invested in their own personal growth and want to discover themselves and who they are in society. This growth also centers around the key areas of emerging adulthood: relationships, employment and education, and worldviews. The key difference for young people on the expedited path is their access to the type of role exploration and experimentation they want to do.

The discussion presented by DeLuca and colleagues produces an important point for reflection for criminologists (including me!) to consider. As we engage with emerging adulthood theory and the arguments it presents, we must examine how well the population of justice-involved young people fit into the baseline expectations and experiences of the theorized emerging adult. Surely, young people in this population may out of necessity be on the "expedited path to adulthood" within some contexts of their lives. Additionally, many are likely to be delayed in their path to adulthood because of the barriers created by justice-system involvement (e.g., Halsey & Deegan, 2015; Massoglia & Uggen, 2010; Salvatore, 2017; Salvatore et al., 2012).

With these considerations, where does that leave the role of emerging adulthood theory and the term "emerging adult" within criminology? In this text, I work to examine if and how the components of emerging adulthood theory can and do apply to justice-involved young people. As evidence in this text will demonstrate, sometimes these young people are on either an expedited path or a delayed path for their emergence into adulthood. Some of these young people also fall within the theorized emerging adulthood path. While all these emerging adults may be emerging at different rates (expedited, delayed, or "on time"), what all these young people have in common is identity projects, and often ones connected with their own desistance process (Maruna, 2001). While these projects are individualized, they all serve as the mechanism for allowing young people to emerge into adulthood. They serve as a bridge in the story of one's maturation between a younger, current, and future self – and as a mechanism for embracing one's desistance.

What Is Desistance?

Criminologists tend to define desistance in one of two ways: either as a process that lasts a while or as the point when someone has ceased engagement in crime. In this text, I favor the former – in that desistance is considered a process by which people begin limiting or ceasing engagement in crime well before their final engagement in crime (Bersani & Doherty, 2018; Bottoms & Shapland, 2011). This text is aimed at understanding the mechanisms that affect emerging adults within their process of desisting. To do this, I explore both the existing literature and provide evidence from qualitative interviews with justice-involved emerging adults (see Chapter 3 for a description of the methods). I work to weave together the empirical data I have gathered with the theorizations, perspectives, and evidence of other scholars to facilitate an interdisciplinary approach to desistance within emerging adulthood.

The desistance process for participants is examined through the changes in behavior they express during their interviews. Thus, participants are self-reporting their own engagement in deviance and crime as well as their desistance from these behaviors. Their desistance processes include their transition out of antisocial, risky, or criminal behaviors and into more prosocial behaviors, identities, and roles. Specifically, for these emerging adults, they express transitioning out of these antisocial or deviant behaviors and into more prosocial behaviors as central to their transition into adulthood. Thus, as these participants are embracing desistance and engaging in various prosocial identity projects, they are limiting their engagement in these antisocial behaviors and instead embracing prosocial adult roles.

Summary of Chapters

Chapter 1 introduces the topic of crime across the life course and outlines the influence of emerging adult theory on life course criminology. This chapter also discusses classical turning points out of crime within the life course and explains how these turning points have changed as a result of structural and cultural shifts in society. Finally, this chapter sets the stage for the need to rethink turning points for emerging adults and introduces this content for the subsequent chapters.

Chapter 2 provides a review of theories of identity and its role in the life course and in desistance. The focus of this chapter is to understand identity theory and the mechanisms behind the identity project and its role in maturation over the life course. This chapter outlines concepts of identity theory across the disciplines of emerging adulthood, developmental psychology, and criminology. These concepts integrate to inform the theoretical framework for the research in this text examining turning points for justice-involved emerging adults.

Chapter 3 presents the methodological approach of this study, which includes a description of the sample, the process of qualitative data collection, and the analytical approach. This chapter also discusses the framework of data collection and analysis under narrative criminology.

Chapter 4 discusses the theoretical concept of maturation and its potential role in bridging the strings of theory across sociology, developmental psychology, and criminology for desistance within emerging adulthood. Further, it also discusses the role of psychological maturation and the identity project in the transition to adulthood and desistance.

Chapters 5 and 6 focus on the social components of maturation. Chapter 5 discusses how relationships and social support function within emerging adulthood. This includes shifts emerging adults experience from adolescence in areas such as romance, family, parenting, and friendship. Chapter 6 examines the shifts in expectations and desires for engaging with social institutions. This includes a discussion on how justice-involved emerging adults perceive the role of employment and civic engagement in their maturation and desistance processes.

The text will conclude with Chapter 7, which offers a discussion of the policy and practice implications of the work presented. The book will conclude by identifying empirically based turning points and strategies to facilitate the success of transitioning out of crime for emerging adults. This chapter will include recommendations for practitioners and policy makers working to serve emerging adults entangled in the justice system to promote successful desistance.

1

THE LIFE COURSE AND EMERGING ADULTHOOD THEORY

The life course perspective was built out of an interdisciplinary understanding that theoretical and empirical contributions from a range of fields were important in studying the process of aging and maturation. There are four overarching stages across the life course: childhood, adolescence, adulthood, and older age. While additional distinctions exist within each of these stages (e.g., infancy as a part of childhood), these four stages represent important categories for socialization and the expectations of social roles that often cross generational and cultural barriers in Western society and research.[1]

Childhood (approximately ages 0–12) is one of the most important stages of the life course as it encompasses some of the most crucial development socially, cognitively, and physically. This stage includes infancy, early childhood, and school-aged childhood. The next major stage is **adolescence** (approximately ages 13–18) where an individual's biological development parallels the exploration of their self, personal identity, and independence. Often, this development is individualized in that it may occur earlier or later for some youth. Adolescence is typically characterized as a transitional stage between puberty and adulthood, where an emphasis lies on preparation for adulthood through risk-taking, exploration, and experimentation.

The longest stage of the life course is **adulthood**, lasting approximately from ages 18 to 64. Adulthood is characterized by establishing stability as an individual embraces their role(s) in society to "settle down", such as starting a career, getting married, and becoming a parent. This stability is facilitated by social, cognitive, and physical development. As young people mature into adulthood, they can embrace the roles typical of an adult and maintain their general position in those roles throughout this stage in the life course.

DOI: 10.4324/9781003143581-2

Importantly, there are several phases within adulthood, including emerging adulthood, young adulthood, and middle age.

The final stage of the life course is **older age** (approximately ages 65 and above). This is classically understood to be a fulfilling point in the life course, where one can reap the benefits of the decisions and stability established throughout the life course. Yet, this stage also welcomes new social, cognitive, and physical challenges as one ages.

The work in this text focuses on **emerging adulthood** (approximately ages 18–29), a transitional stage between adolescence and adulthood characterized by prolonged engagement in adolescent-type behaviors (e.g., risk-taking, exploration, and experimentation) within the realm of adulthood (Arnett, 2000, 2015, 2016). As this chapter will discuss, emerging adulthood creates a unique opportunity for prolonged engagement in deviance and its crucial effects on how young people can engage in desistance. To set the context for the rest of this text, this chapter will provide a introduction to the fundamental perspectives within developmental and life course criminology as well as emerging adulthood theory.

But First, a Primer on Structure Versus Agency

As a field, developmental and life course criminology focuses on the engagement in offending and desistance across one's life course. Theories under this perspective tend to favor either structurally-based factors, agentic-based factors, or an integration between the two. Structurally-based perspectives in criminology are typically concerned with theorizing the role of social factors, including social structure and life events, in the offending and desistance processes. Theoretical frameworks under this perspective argue that desistance from crime is a result of changes in social, structural, or environmental factors. Crime (and behaviors in general) are affected by the social-structural factors that an individual may be exposed to, such as socioeconomic stratifications, social institutions (e.g., government, education), communities and social (or peer) networks, and cultural norms (Laub & Sampson, 2003; Lopez & Scott, 2000; Murdock, 1949; Sampson & Laub, 1993).

Agentic-based perspectives in criminology are typically concerned with theorizing the role of individual factors, including psychological and biological factors, in the developmental process and engagement of crime. Theoretical frameworks under this perspective argue that desistance from crime is a result of an individual realizing that involvement in criminal or antisocial activities is no longer worth the costs. A person then begins to fear for their future and subsequently works to embrace a prosocial pathway for their life course (Giordano et al., 2002; Maruna, 2001). Agentic-based theories argue that people believe they are in control of their own decisions, the outcomes of said decisions, the course of their lives, and how they react to obstacles that may arise (Côté & Levine, 2002; Schwartz et al., 2005).

Developmental and Life Course Criminology

The relationship between age and crime is considered one of the most established features in the field of criminology. Typically, the **age-crime curve** presents an aggregate view of crime rates or crime counts by age, visualizing a peak in the occurrence of crime during the mid- to late-teens followed by a swift decline in the early to mid-20s. In their work, Hirschi and Gottfredson (1983; Gottfredson & Hirschi 1990) argue that this peak is approximately similar across various crime types and types of data (e.g., arrest and victimization). This curvilinear relationship, which peaks within late adolescence or early adulthood, persists across demographic characteristics and across time (Rocque, 2017).

Since the identification of this curve, many scholars have dedicated their life's work to theorizing why this age-crime curve exists and identifying the mechanisms behind it. Two of the most influential theoretical approaches in the field are those of Moffitt's Dual Taxonomy and Sampson and Laub's age-graded informal social control theory:

1 Moffitt's Dual Taxonomy (1993) is a developmental perspective that argues that deviance begins and peaks within the life stage of adolescence. Once a young person ages out of adolescence, they reduce or stop their engagement in deviance.
2 Sampson and Laub (1993; Laub & Sampson 2003) take a life course perspective connecting social controls (e.g., attachment to family and friends; involvement in school or work; belief in the law) to a change in behaviors across the life course. Under this perspective, social controls are the key to understanding when the risk of deviance is highest for young people.

Moffitt's Dual Taxonomy

Moffit's (1993) dual taxonomy of offending presents two trajectories for deviance: the *adolescent-limited* and the *life course persistent*.[2] The **adolescent-limited** trajectory is typically defined by engagement in lower-level crimes, such as shoplifting and vandalism, or status offenses such as underage drinking. The majority of young people engaging in deviance or crime are theorized to fall into this trajectory, where they generally desist from deviance and crime once they reach adulthood in their late-teens and early 20s. Moffitt explains that this adolescent-limited trajectory results from the delay between biological and social maturation, where adolescents engage in offending and other antisocial behaviors due to the frustration experienced by being biologically mature but not socially mature.

This gap between biological and social maturation creates a dissonance between how young people may feel and how they are viewed by others in society. As biological maturity is reached in adolescence, young people are asked to delay their engagement in conventional adult roles, such as marriage, parenting, establishing a career, voting and civic engagement, or alcohol use. Thus, adolescents seek alternative ways to mimic or engage in adult behaviors (Moffitt, 1993; see Greenberg, 1977). Adolescents eventually can reconcile the maturity gap that exists between their biological maturity and their social status through their engagement in conventional adult roles, decreasing the need to engage in risky behaviors like criminal offending (Moffitt, 1993; see also Barnes & Beaver, 2010; Piquero & Brezina, 2001).

While young people who fall into the **life course persistent** trajectory also engage in lower-level crimes and status offenses, they additionally engage in more serious crimes such as violence or illegal drug use. Moffitt (1993) explains that those in the life course persistent trajectory may start engagement in deviance and crime at a younger age and continue to do so throughout adulthood. This engagement can be amplified by "high-risk" social environments, including poverty/economic hardship and poor relationships with family, peers, teachers, partners, and employers (Moffitt et al., 2002). The antisocial or risky behaviors of the life course persistent group will manifest and thus compound across several domains (e.g., relationships, workplace, community), affecting the transitions out of adolescence and into adulthood (Elder, 1998; Moffit et al., 2002). Young people in this trajectory, thus, may face greater barriers in their desistance processes compared to their peers in the adolescent-limited trajectory.

Sampson and Laub's Age-Graded Social Controls

Sampson and Laub's work on the life course over the years (Laub et al., 2018; Laub & Sampson, 2003; Sampson & Laub, 1993) builds from the theoretical understanding that the life course is sectioned across developmental stages, with variations in formal and informal social controls across these stages. Through their age-graded theory, Sampson and Laub argue that as an individual ages through society, their (formal and informal) bonds to society change. Salient life events (i.e., **turning points**) and socialization across the life course can impact one's trajectory of behavior, potentially pushing them toward or away from crime. Thus, theoretical turning points in the life course stem from creating formal and informal social bonds through prosocial institutions such as marriage, employment, joining the military, or parenting (see Laub et al., 2018; Laub & Sampson, 2003; Sampson & Laub, 1993).

Similar to Moffitt's taxonomy, and many other life course perspectives, Sampson and Laub acknowledge that adolescents are in a phase of the life course that is optimal for engagement in risky behaviors, deviance, and low-level crime. As adolescents age into adulthood, they are able to embrace turning points. These turning points serve as mechanisms for desistance, providing young people with a framework for and opportunities to engage with social controls that facilitate the aging out of risky behaviors and investing in prosocial adulthood (Farrington & West, 1995; Sampson & Laub, 1993). Conversely, those who do not experience turning points and do not establish prosocial bonds with formal institutions and informal bonds within social networks are at a greater risk of engaging in risky behaviors as adults.

Turning Points as "Hooks for Change"

Turning points function as "hooks for change" in that they serve as catalysts for changes within the life course (Giordano et al., 2002, 2007). Turning points present an opportunity to move away from previous behaviors (e.g., crime) and statuses (e.g., juvenile delinquent) to embrace new pathways and behaviors in the life course (Elder, 1986; Sampson & Laub, 1993). As young people age and mature, their place in society shifts allowing for transitions in and out of risky behaviors. Under this perspective, desistance from deviant behaviors functions as a process across the life course (Bersani & Doherty, 2018; Bushway et al., 2003; Kazemian, 2007; Laub & Sampson, 2001; Maruna, 2001). As a young person moves through the life course, new turning points and contexts for social bonds can facilitate the processes of desistance. These turning points simultaneously facilitate the transition into adulthood, allowing young people to see themselves in adult roles in society (Arnett, 1998, 2006; Tanner & Arnett, 2009). Those who are open to the "hooks for change" can build a new identity through the turning points they embrace (Giordano et al., 2002). Therefore, turning points provide an opportunity for young people to create a new beginning, with the possibility for new experiences and personal growth.

While there are several possibilities of what encompasses turning points, the literature identifies five common categories that are used to codify the transition into adulthood: (1) establishing an independent household from parents/family, (2) completion of education, (3) employment, (4) marriage/relationships, and (5) having children (Berlin et al., 2010; Furstenberg, 2006, 2008, 2010; Furstenberg et al., 2005; Lee & Waithaka, 2017; Settersten & Ray, 2010). Additionally, literature within developmental psychology has argued that certain "qualities" can function as turning points for the transition into adulthood. Often when young people embrace these "qualities", such as accepting responsibility for one's actions, making independent decisions, and gaining financial independence, they can similarly mark the transition into adulthood (Arnett, 1998, 2006).

One classic example of a turning point is joining the military, where young people can sever themselves from the adult social role expectation of entering a traditional career in the efforts of establishing a new beginning (see Elder, 1986, 1998). This developmental turning point provides a specific opportunity in which young people can embrace personal change, taking a break from societal expectations (e.g., entering the workforce at 18) to develop a new trajectory for their life course (Laub & Sampson, 2003). However, several contemporary tests have found more limited support for this turning point in facilitating desistance (Bouffard, 2005; Craig & Foster, 2013). This emphasizes that turning points are not necessarily universal to all youth, and especially not across generational contexts.

The availability of turning points is also constrained by the structural factors (e.g., relationships, gender, race/ethnicity, socioeconomic status) that interact with them, limiting the availability of social identities, and thus the opportunity to transition into new identities (Giordano et al., 2002, 2007). The timing of these turning points in the life course, as well as the severity of deviance, may also play an important role in how turning points function within the desistance processes of young people (Uggen, 2000). Ultimately, it is important to understand what influences the transition into adulthood for justice-involved young people (Arnett, 2007; Furstenberg et al., 2005; Massoglia & Uggen, 2010) and if the nature of adult roles (i.e., turning points) for this population can successfully facilitate desistance for modern-day young people (Hill et al., 2016).

Socio-Structural Changes in Society

As a result of socio-structural changes in society, how young people access or are expected to access turning points has shifted. Changes to the economy, job market, and social norms (e.g., the average age of marriage or parenthood) influence when turning points are experienced and how their importance is interpreted. These shifts include a delayed onset of marriage and parenting, seeking a meaningful career, an emphasis on pursuing higher education, and embracing identity exploration (e.g., Arnett, 2000, 2016; Shanahan, 2000; Vespa, 2017). As a result, scholars acknowledge that traditional adulthood markers (e.g., marriage, parenting, employment) are not reached until the later 20s and early 30s (Furstenberg et al., 2005).

Consequently, the understanding of the relationship between age, turning points, and desistance must shift accordingly (Massoglia & Uggen, 2010). Young people may not be able to age out of crime as previously conceptualized because of the structural changes (e.g., changes in the economy, emphasis on higher education, shifts in cultural norms) and demographic shifts (e.g., increased age of marriage, increased age of parenthood) within Western society. Many of these structural changes notably impede the agency young people have in society and the expectations of when and what markers are achieved to facilitate a transition into adult roles.

Ultimately, this has led to a prolonged engagement in adolescent-type behaviors within the life course stage of adulthood. This creates new contexts for how young people work to reconcile the maturity gap that inhibits their full participation in conventional adult society. For example, young people are considered legal adults at the age of 18 and given certain rights and responsibilities, like being able to vote. However, young people are still asked to delay other aspects of adult life, such as alcohol use at age 21, the expectation of continuing education until around age 22, and waiting to get married and raise children until after education is completed and a career has been secured. Thus, young people are often forced to remain financially and socially dependent on their family or parents into the beginning of this phase of adulthood. However, they want to engage in their own intimate relationships, establish their own homes and collect their own belongings, make their own decisions, and be viewed and accepted as adults (Moffitt, 1993). For emerging adults, the turning points they can access are often only considered temporary, threatening the successful transition into adulthood. Consequently, these emerging adults are still "trapped in a *maturity gap*, chronological hostages of a time warp between biological age and social age" (Moffitt, 1993, p. 687).

As discussed in the introduction, research on the impact of these socio-structural shifts on adolescent development has led scholars to delineate the period of **emerging adulthood**. The life course phase of emerging adulthood is characterized by role exploration throughout the late teens and 20s, whereby young people can investigate the potential trajectories of their lives prior to committing to finalized adult roles (Arnett, 2000). Emerging adults, thus, view traditional adulthood markers as temporary roles through which they can explore and experiment, including in the contexts of relationships, careers, and worldviews. This affords emerging adults an opportunity of normalized identity exploration and transformation so that they can discover "who they are" (Arnett, 1997; Mayseless & Scharf, 2003; Vignoles, 2018).

Emerging Adulthood Theory

Arnett, in his seminal work (2000), developed emerging adulthood theory to understand how socio-structural changes in society have influenced development across the life course for modern-day young people. Arnett presents emerging adulthood as a developmental stage from the late teens through the late 20s, where the transition into adult roles continues into the late 20s and even early 30s (Arnett, 2000; 2016). Emerging adulthood theory proposes that this stage in the life course for young people is characterized by their engagement in identity exploration, instability, self-focus, and embracement of possibility for their futures. While within this stage, young people often feel in-between adolescence and adulthood, recognizing that they have left the stage of adolescence behind but not quite feeling like a complete adult (Arnett, 2000; 2016). Therefore, this stage is one where young people have "left the dependency of childhood and adolescence" but have "not yet entered the enduring responsibilities that are normative of adulthood" (Arnett, 2000, p. 469).

Throughout emerging adulthood, young people are actively engaging in role exploration and identity transformation in order to establish an adult self (Luyckx et al., 2006). As a result of delayed expectations of when traditional adulthood markers are to be reached, emerging adults, thus, view roles in this life stage as temporary—or ones they can explore and experiment with. This affords emerging adults an opportunity for normalized identity exploration and transformation so that they can discover "who they are" (Arnett, 1997; Mayseless & Scharf, 2003; Vignoles, 2018). Because of this acceptable (and encouraged) period of exploration, young people do not commit to adult roles until later in the life course compared to previous generations. The effects of these delayed expectations and continued identity exploration are pervasive within the Millennial generation and continuing with Generation Z, creating a marked shift in the maturation process caused by the socio-structural conditions under which these generations are growing up.

As young people age into their late teens and early 20s, their experiences with and expectations of social and structural institutions change. For example, while adolescents of previous generations may engage in identity and role exploration prior to the age of 18, they get to do so under the purview of parents and the education system. Emerging adults experiences shifts to the social bonds typical of their adolescence, including the shift from mandatory schooling to an emphasis on establishing a career or attending college (Arnett, 2004), autonomy from parents (Dubas & Petersen, 1996), and a new setting for reliance on peers (Allan, 2008). Therefore, the context of identity and role exploration for young people in these generations is distinct from that theorized of adolescents from previous generations.

In addition, environmental barriers (e.g., job market, economic stability, recessions) may impede the ability of emerging adults to attain traditional adulthood roles, such as stable employment and home ownership (Côté & Bynner, 2008; Salvatore & Taniguchi, 2012). These changes are coupled with new structures of social controls, as emerging adults are no longer subject to the purview of others (e.g., teachers) and often have new relationships with peers and parents (Salvatore, 2017). Societal changes provide emerging adults with a unique opportunity for greater social freedom, which may encourage engagement in risky behaviors. The delays in these traditional adult roles among emerging adults suggest that they require reconceptualization.

Emerging adulthood theory also theorizes that emerging adults view values relating to the quality of character as among the most important markers in their transition into adulthood. Qualities of character such as accepting responsibility for oneself, making independent decisions, and becoming financially independent may be considered more important than existing markers of traditional adulthood (e.g., marriage, parenthood, career) for those who have not yet attained these markers (Arnett, 1997, 1998, 2000; Greene et al., 1992; Scheer et al., 1996). This is especially evident in the workplace, as emerging adults view their career as an opportunity for self-expression, fulfillment, and enjoyment, which was not seen in earlier generations (Arnett, 2004). Traditional values of earlier generations (e.g., work is unpleasant but necessary) may not apply within emerging adulthood, resulting in changes to the functioning of the accompanying adulthood markers (Arnett, 2015).

Role Exploration in Emerging Adulthood

Emerging adults are typically not focused on establishing their finalized adult role within this life stage. Instead, this stage provides an opportunity for them to explore various roles prior to settling into a lasting adult role (Arnett, 2000). This allows emerging adults to acquire a wide variety of experiences prior to the limitations of finalized adult roles.[3] This is especially appealing for those who wish to experience a variety of romantic relationships or sexual experiences prior to marriage or those who wish to try out a variety of work or educational programs, including unique short-term opportunities or those that include traveling/moving somewhere new (Arnett, 2000). Researchers have highlighted three main areas of role exploration within emerging adulthood: relationships, careers, and worldviews.

First, relationships are important in emerging adulthood, just as they are for many other stages across the life course. Specifically, romantic relationships may be some of the most important during this time. While many young people may begin dating during adolescence, they still view this period of dating as primarily recreational (Arnett, 2000; Roscoe et al., 1987) and temporary, allowing for the exploration of romantic love and sexual experiences (Arnett, 2000; Feiring, 1996). Romantic experiences in adolescence are often shorter and may exist within the context of social activities such as parties and dances (Arnett, 2000). In the transition into emerging adulthood, romantic explorations become more intimate, with the focus shifting toward physical and emotional intimacy. These relationships tend to last longer and may involve cohabitation, with the focus shifting toward intimacy and exploring the qualities and characteristics desired of a life partner (Arnett, 2000; Shulman & Connolly, 2016).

Distinct changes also occur in the context of familial relationships as emerging adults often seek autonomy and independence from their parents and families. Autonomy in the relationship between emerging adults and their parents (e.g., not living with parents, not being financially reliant on parents) is an important marker for the transition out of adolescence (Arnett, 2000, 2016). Because of the contexts of emerging adulthood, young people are delayed in succeeding in establishing this independence from parents and family as they remain fiscally and socially reliant on their families in the absence of other turning points (e.g., marriage, homeownership). Yet, establishing this autonomy and independence improves the relationship between the emerging adult and their parent (Dubas & Petersen, 1996; Fingerman & Yahirun, 2016; O'Connor et al., 1996).

While relationships with peers remain important for emerging adults, the expectations and needs of these relationships change for this period of the life course. Friendships and the support they provide are important in encouraging young people as they adapt to the transition to adulthood (Barry et al., 2016). Friends often fill the gap created during role exploration between the childhood family and establishing an adult family (via partnership and potential parenthood), often making peer groups the primary support for emerging adults (Allan, 2008). The importance of friendship and the potential change of peer groups during the exploration within emerging adulthood are important indicators of the developmental process (Barry et al., 2016), reflecting potential changes in social roles (Carstensen et al., 1999).

Second is the career, an adult role that significantly influences the identity. While many adolescents may be employed part-time, they often seek these positions to pay for leisurely activities such as clothing, concerts, or eating out (Bachman & Schulenberg, 1993; Shanahan et al., 1996). Often this work is in the service industry, with jobs at restaurants, retail stores, and seasonal positions during school breaks. Although adolescents acknowledge that having such positions may help them learn how to manage their time and money (Mortimer et al., 1999), they are generally not positions that provide them with the knowledge, skills, or preparation for their future careers (Arnett, 2000; Greenberger & Steinberg, 1986).

Emerging adulthood, in contrast, represents a time in the life course where work experiences are more directly related to preparation for a future career. Emerging adults can explore various work possibilities to gain knowledge and learn skills that will help prepare them for the foundation of their career (Arnett, 2000; Dietrich & Salmela-Aro, 2016; Marshall & Butler, 2016). Additionally, emerging adults explore potential career trajectories with the goal of establishing meaningful and satisfying employment (Arnett, 2004). This is echoed by the increased emphasis on higher education, where college students can utilize their education to explore different majors and consider potential occupational trajectories (Arnett, 2000; Magolda & Taylor, 2016; Marshall & Butler, 2016).

Finally, within the period of emerging adulthood, worldviews and changes within them are central to cognitive development (King & Kitchener, 2016; Perry, 1999). Worldview exploration includes the reexamination of beliefs and values learned through family and social institutions (e.g., religion, school, community) in an effort of autonomous reflection to build one's own belief system (Arnett & Jensen, 2002; Hoge et al., 1993). This process contributes to moral development within emerging adulthood, where one must begin to consider their values and belief system in relation to their own behaviors (Padilla-Walker, 2016). As young people become exposed to a variety of worldviews in their adult lives, this often leads them to question their own preexisting perspectives (Arnett, 2000). Emerging adults typically remain open to adjusting and refining their world view throughout this life stage, acknowledging the importance of establishing their own beliefs and values as a part of the process of cognitive maturation into adulthood (Arnett, 1997; King & Kitchener, 2016).

Exploration across these three areas (i.e., relationships, careers, and worldviews) provides a specific opportunity for justice-involved emerging adults to embrace prosocial roles and transition into desistance from crime or other antisocial behaviors. For example, justice-involved emerging adults can sever ties with antisocial peers and begin to build networks of prosocial peers, which may be necessary for desistance (e.g., Giordano et al., 2002; Kiecolt, 1994). Additionally, engaging in meaningful and fulfilling employment may reduce participation in crime or other antisocial behaviors (e.g., Porfeli et al., 2011; Uggen, 2000). Establishing new worldviews may also support desistance from criminal or risky behaviors, such as drug use or violence. Therefore, life course criminologists must consider how concepts within emerging adulthood apply to the process of desistance among justice-involved emerging adults.

Bridging Emerging Adulthood Theory and Life Course Criminology

Certainly, criminologists have engaged with emerging adult theory and emerging adult researchers have engaged criminological theory in their efforts to understand crime, deviance, and desistance across the life course. This interdisciplinary research has identified peaks in crime within emerging adulthood, including arrest rates (e.g., Piquero et al., 2002), substance use (e.g., Arnett, 1998; Bachman et al., 2014), and violence or aggressive behaviors (e.g., Marcus, 2009). For example, many adolescents (both justice- and not justice-involved) engage in substance use, including alcohol consumption, marijuana use, and use of other illicit drugs (Johnston et al., 2010). Substance use continues during the early to mid-20s as young people explore different identities, because they view such behavior as age-appropriate (especially when among peers), and because they may seek the sensation of this substance use (Arnett, 2005). As young people age (typically around age 30) and embrace adult social roles, they tend to reduce engaging in substance use (Bachman et al., 2014).

Interdisciplinary works such as these acknowledge that gaps persist within traditional criminological perspectives in examining the desistance process among younger adults. These gaps largely overlap with the main characteristics of emerging adulthood theory, and criminologists have encouraged integrating emerging adulthood theory into preexisting perspectives to examine how young people engage in desistance as they face delays or barriers in achieving traditional turning points and markers of adulthood (Halsey & Deegan, 2015; Nader, 2019; Nader & Davies Robinson, 2023; Salvatore, 2017).

For example, these delays in achieving adulthood may be affecting how Moffitt's offending trajectories currently function. Emerging adults may be engaging in antisocial and criminal behaviors longer than proposed by Moffitt (1993) as a result of the delays in the transitions into adult roles (i.e., turning points). The gap left in these trajectories by emerging adulthood may mean that the adolescent-limited phase of offending is prolonged (Massoglia & Uggen, 2010; Salvatore et al., 2012). Salvatore and colleagues (2012) even proposed that the "prolonged adolescent" offender trajectory from ages 18 to 25 may exist within Moffit's (1993) taxonomy for those who have failed to transition into adult social roles, continue to engage in antisocial/criminal behaviors, and lack strong bonds to conventional society. Emerging adults who continue to persist in antisocial or risky behaviors (including lower-level offenses) and lack conventional social bonds to society may be caught in the maturity gap longer than those in the traditionally conceptualized adolescent-limited trajectory (Salvatore et al., 2012). Researchers, therefore, must reconsider theoretical perspectives that apply to those that fall within this gap of the life course.

Conclusion

The life course perspective inherently encompasses an interdisciplinary approach to studying the processes of aging and maturation. As this chapter reviewed, emerging adulthood has become an accepted stage in the life course for modern-day young people. Emerging adulthood is characterized as a transitional stage between adolescence and adulthood where young people prolong their engagement in behaviors typical of adolescence into during the earliest years of adulthood. These include activities such as role exploration, identity transformation, and experimentation. The context and characteristics of emerging adulthood facilitate a period of instability that a young adult can capitalize on to explore their provisional role in society and their self-perceptions.

Consequentially, emerging adulthood may prolong the maturity gap in the life course of risk-taking and deviance that previous generations of youth typically aged out of. Researchers, thus, need to examine how young and emerging adults engage in desistance under the context of new social norms, turning points, and "hooks" for change. A large part of how young people engage in this process rests in their identity development and maturation. Who a young person sees themselves as, or who they want to become, are important cognitive drivers linked with changes in behavior. Yet, the socio-structural context of emerging adulthood has shifted how young people can embrace identity projects and access turning points to facilitate desistance.

Notes

1 For further discussion, see Mortimer and Shanahan (2007) and Shanahan et al. (2016).
2 It is important to note that nuances exist to this perspective and how trajectories of crime and desistance function for adolescents and young people. For further discussion, see: Nagin et al. (1995) and Nagin (2005).
3 It is important to note that adults are able to explore and change within roles and identities throughout the life course. The "finalized" adult roles discussed here refer to those roles that are indicative of the transition from emerging adulthood into either "young adulthood" or adulthood.

2

THEORIZING IDENTITY AND MATURATION

At the crux of developmental and life course criminology and emerging adulthood is the concept of reaching adulthood. Both fields argue that the process of transitioning into adulthood affects behavior and choices. Importantly though, aging itself must not be conflated with maturation. In line with the work of Glueck and Glueck (1937, 1940; see also Rocque, 2015), I consider maturation as a process that occurs across the life course of young adults where they develop across biological, psychological, and social domains. Thus, while aging biologically may be one component of the maturation process, psychological and social maturation are separate processes that are engaged during development. The psychological and social domains focus on "who" someone "is" – or their identity both personally and socially.

The fields of criminology and emerging adulthood take different approaches to theorizing identity and its role in the maturation process. In this chapter, I examine these theorizations of identities. For young people, this stage in the life course is focused on understanding who they are and where they see themselves in society (Arnett, 2000; Côté, 2002; Klimstra et al., 2010; Luyckx et al., 2006). This exploration and meaning-making defines how they make choices, form relationships, and act in society. Thus, this chapter will take an interdisciplinary approach, leveraging the work of scholars across several fields to (1) explore identity theory, (2) contextualize this within emerging adulthood, and (3) discuss the process of growing up (or the maturation of identity).

As many terms do, **identity** takes on various conceptualizations across interdisciplinary research in psychology, sociology, and criminology. Identity is a multidimensional concept, associated with different meanings across

DOI: 10.4324/9781003143581-3

various research projects and dimensions of analysis. Identity is studied at the psychological, interactional, and societal levels, and within each of these levels exists variations (see Côté, 2015, for further discussion). As an author, I must recognize this and communicate to you, the reader, the meaning of identity in the context of this text. The goal of this is not to dismiss other perspectives of identity theory but to set the stage for how identity is theorized to play a role in this text.

In the case of this work, the identity being discussed is within the circumstances of the transition to adulthood. Young people can develop and form specific personal and social identities that make them feel as though they have reached a level of adulthood in society or become perceived as if they have. This chapter examines what identity is theoretically, how identities can be formed, and the function of identity within the transition to adulthood. This chapter, and the subsequent content of the book, will engage with identity in both a psychological perspective personal to the individual and social perspective for how the individual fits into social systems and institutions.

Identity Theory

APA's Dictionary of Psychology (2015) defines **identity**, or personal identity, as:

> an individual's sense of self defined by (a) a set of physical, psychological, and interpersonal characteristics that is not wholly shared with any other person and (b) a range of affiliations (e.g., ethnicity) and social roles. Identity involves a sense of continuity, or the feeling that one is the same person today that one was yesterday or last year (despite physical or other changes). Such a sense is derived from one's body sensations; one's body image; and the feeling that one's memories, goals, values, expectations, and beliefs belong to the self.

Bamberg (2011) provides a deep dive into the concept of identity, and its position in theory and research. Every individual has one or more identities that they believe represent "who" they "are". Identities offer a way to "differentiate and integrate [our] sense of self " into various social and personal situations (Bamberg, 2011, p. 6). These identities can be a combination of self-image/self-perception and the perceptions of others, and bridge various socio-structural facets of life, including gender, race/ethnicity, age, occupation, religion, moral facets, and beyond.

Often, when identities are assigned to us either by ourselves or by others, they are difficult or impossible to lose (Bamberg, 2011). Some identities, such as race or ethnicity, are considered to be unchangeable. But generally, most types of identities can change and often do as we progress through the life course, participate in different social settings, and engage with various world structures. Identities help to provide a structure of one's self-perception, as well as consistency and coherence to one's beliefs, goals, and self across the life course (Adams & Marshall, 1996). Each identity we possess must tackle three quandaries, as defined by Bamberg (2011, p. 6)

i sameness of a sense of self across time in the face of constant change;
ii uniqueness of the person vis-à-vis others in the face of being the same as everyone else; and
iii the construction of agency as constituted by self (with a self-to-world direction of fit) and world (with a world-to-self direction of fit)

Thus, Bamberg argues that identity begins from the continuity of the self-change dilemma. From here, identity then can be affected by our uniqueness from others (individuality) and agency to change our identity. In this process of asking "Who am I?", people can engage reflexivity and take an active role in the construction and change of their own identities.

A person's identities are related to the various roles they can play in society (Burke & Stets, 2009; Vignoles, 2018). Typically, individuals may have many identities that come together to construct the greater *self*, or internal view a person has of themselves. These identities exist, and vary, both personally (i.e., within the individual) and socially (i.e., to others, see Vignoles, 2018). Together, our personal and social identities construct a full sense of "who one is" (Paternoster & Bushway, 2009, p. 1111; see also Vignoles et al., 2011). As personal and social identities change and warp, in turn, the perception of one's *self*-image changes with it.

When undergoing a change in identity, reflection on the past self can facilitate adjustments to one's approach toward the future (Vaughan, 2007; see also Goldie, 2003). Individuals can enact purposeful actions that aid in altering their sense of self (Kiecolt, 1994; Rocque et al., 2016). This understanding of identity has been important in the development of criminological research on agency and desistance. This work argues that desistance may result from an individual's perception of their responsibility for their own decisions, the course of their life, and the outcomes of their decisions (Côté & Levine, 2002; Maruna, 2001; Paternoster & Bushway, 2009; Schwartz et al., 2005).

Dimensions of Identity Development

To situate identity theory within the context of the life course, I must first review theories on identity development. Identity development, formation, and maintenance all center around building, adjusting, and embracing of identities in both personal and social contexts. Current models for identity development largely build on the work of Erikson's (1968) theory of identity development and Marcia's (1966, 1980) work on identity statuses. Erikson argued that identity development was the central crisis of development, particularly during the life stage of adolescence. In adolescence, young people exist in a **psychosocial moratorium** where they do not commit to any specific roles or identities, but instead experiment and explore various identities and roles. This experimentation is an attempt to find one's unique identity and place within social systems. (Erikson, 1968). As a result of exploring various roles and opportunities in society, youth can commit to the identities or roles of their choice.

Erikson (1968) argued that identity development bridges an adolescent between their past (i.e., childhood) and their future (i.e., adulthood). When an identity is (or multiple identities are) formed, it serves as a marker for successful development and transition in the life course. Erikson termed this as **identity achievement**, and when youth reach identity achievement, they have created this bridge into adulthood. With identity achievement comes a coherent view of one's self – an understanding of "who one is". If youth fail to commit to developing an identity, they perpetuate their existence in the psychosocial moratorium, delaying or failing to construct their bridge into adulthood. Their role in society, thus, becomes unclear and their participation in social systems is threatened.

Marica's (1966, 1980) work expands on Erikson's theory by breaking down the concepts of exploration and commitment for adolescents and embracing the nuances of each of these dimensions. Table 2.1 presents Marcia's four identity statuses and where each of these statuses falls onto the two dimensions of exploration and commitment. The first two identity statuses, identity achievement and identity moratorium, operate under Erikson's (1968) theory that youth engage in high levels of identity exploration. Those who engage in high levels of identity exploration and commit to an identity after this exploration period fall into the status of identity achievement. Those who engage in high levels of identity exploration but do not commit to an identity after this exploration period fall into the status of identity moratorium.

Marica's expansion on Erikson's work primarily focuses on acknowledging that not all youth have the same opportunity or desire to explore their identity options. For some youth, a variety of exploration opportunities

TABLE 2.1 Marica's (1966, 1980) Four Identity Statuses

		Exploration of identity options	
		High	*Low*
Commitment to identity	Yes	Identity Achievement	Identity Foreclosure
	No	Identity Moratorium	Identity Diffusion

are not provided and may be limited as a result of their social context (e.g., family, friends) or structural factors (e.g., school system, where they live). This echoes the concerns of DeLuca and colleagues (2016) discussed in the introduction on the applicability of the term *emerging* in emerging adulthood. Not all youth will have the socio-structural context to engage in identity exploration, and instead may be on an *expedited* path to identity commitment regardless of their desire to explore. When young people engage only in a low level of identity exploration, either by their own volition or as determined by their socio-structural context, they can still either commit or not commit to the limited identities available to them. For those youth who engage in low levels of identity exploration but still commit to an identity, they fall into **identity foreclosure**. Those youth who engage in low levels of identity exploration and do not commit to an identity, fall into **identity diffusion**.

Under Marcia's perspective (1966, 1980), young people who fall into identity foreclosure have committed to an identity without exploring all of their available options. This may be a result of pressures from parents, peers, or cultural expectations and, often, this dimension is characteristic of younger adolescents who may choose a preliminary identity out of anxiety or social pressure. Parents may even make these identity choices for their children without providing them with any opportunity to explore options. Some youth may even just model the identities of those they admire or identify with and accept these identities observed in their role models. However, Marcia argues most adolescents likely mature out of the foreclosure dimension as they grow older and eventually begin to explore more identity options.

Young people who fall into identity diffusion have not explored or committed to any identity options (Marcia, 1966, 1980). This may be a result of young people being unfamiliar with the identity formation process – they may have limited experience with or awareness of their opportunity to explore identities and may also have little expectation for the need to commit to an identity. Young people in this category may be restricted in the opportunities available to them socially or structurally and may not have the agency to begin this type of exploration or commitment in their adolescence. However, most adolescents are likely to grow out of this stage as they become exposed to new experiences and potential role models. Marcia concludes that those youth who persist in this dimension past adolescence may feel very little connection to themselves and their place in society.

Since the works of Erikson and Marcia, researchers have determined that the achievement of the identity is rarely completed at the end of adolescence (Arnett, 2000; Côté, 2006; Waterman, 1982). Identity and role exploration continues into the late teens and through the 20s for emerging adults (Arnett, 2000; Luyckx et al., 2006). As young people continue to be exposed to new experiences and engage in higher levels of role exploration, they naturally progress from identity diffusion and foreclosure into identity moratorium and achievement.

As emerging adulthood is characterized by its role exploration and experimentation, it serves as a breeding ground for identity moratorium. Often, young people in this life phase are encouraged to be in this moratorium as it facilitates identity exploration, potentially pulling them out of the categories of foreclosure and diffusion. This moratorium also bridges access into identity achievement as young people engage in role exploration and latch onto roles that resonate with them. This allows emerging adults to develop an individualized pathway for becoming an adult when and how they want to under Marcia's identity statuses.

Identity Content Versus Identity Processes

Two components of identity are identified as necessary for understanding identity development: content and process (see McLean et al., 2016a; McLean et al., 2016b; Syed & Azmitia, 2010; Syed & McLean, 2016). The first component, **identity content**, refers to the *what* of identity, or the type of identity that is being developed. This content of identity relates to how one may see themselves or want to see themselves, including identities or roles one associates with when they think about "who they are". Thus, the content of identity development offers context for the identity – in terms of the circumstances under which the identity can develop. The second component, **identity process**, refers to the *how* of identity being developed. This includes the activities and experiences that an individual engages in that relate to their identity. Drawing connections between one's actions and the meaning behind these actions can provide a foundation for prosocial identity development.

In their work, McLean and colleagues (McLean et al. 2016a; McLean et al., 2016b) argue that identity scholars largely focus on the process of identity development, and ignore the content of the identity being developed. This focus is understandable for scholars in developmental psychology whose field focuses on understanding how people develop. However, for criminologists and sociologists to truly understand identity development in the context of their research, these scholars must work to understand what identity is being developed, which requires studying both what is meaningful to the individual and how this is put into practice to build a new identity (Syed & McLean, 2016; see also Frisen & Wängqvist, 2011; McLean et al., 2016b). McLean and colleagues also emphasize that this argument is both not novel (see Kroger & Marcia, 2011) and in line with Erikson's (1968) theoretical argument that "examining content allows us to see how identity processes are (or are not) employed to integrate various aspects of the self" (McLean et al., 2016a, p. 356). Importantly, this echoes the arguments of DeLuca and colleagues (2016) that researchers need to understand the barriers imposed by the socio-structural context a young person experiences prior to and during their transition to adulthood.

Agency

Within this realm of the study of identity, identity change requires the engagement of agency. Here, the term **agency** refers to the level of active pursuit of opportunities that will facilitate individual growth across many dimensions of the life course (e.g., occupational, intellectual, psychosocial; see Maruna, 2001; Schwartz et al., 2005). Both criminologists and developmental psychologists have discussed the function of agency for identity change within their respective fields. These conceptualizations of agency's role in identity change mesh together very well – and offer a path for theory integration across these interdisciplinary perspectives.

Identity scholars studying emerging adulthood have theorized agency as the responsibility emerging adults perceive that they have over the course of their own life, including the belief that they control their own decisions and are responsible for their own outcomes (Côté & Levine, 2002; Schwartz et al., 2005). These scholars emphasize that for emerging adults to access agency, they must recognize their role or ability in overcoming life's obstacles. While this concept may function well for the average emerging adult's obstacles (i.e., dealing with college, employment, interpersonal problems, or deciding where to head on vacation), this poses a problem for emerging adults who face socio-structural barriers (DeLuca et al., 2016). Realistically, and rationally, those involved in the justice system may feel that they do not have the agency to overcome the consequences of justice system involvement, including being incarcerated or having a criminal record.

Therefore, to truly understand the process of identity development, we must consider both what identity is developing and how it is developed by a person (McLean et al., 2016a; Syed & McLean, 2016). The processes (i.e., activities) involved in undergoing identity development must be understood within contexts (i.e., situations, circumstances, domains, and environments) that are meaningful to the person who is developing their identity (Kroger & Marcia, 2011; McLean et al., 2016b). This allows for the understanding of which identity processes are or are not utilized to integrate a cohesive view of the self (Erikson, 1968; McLean et al., 2016b). Ultimately, research on identity development among justice-involved emerging adults must consider the context and implications of justice-system involvement on identity development, including understanding the barriers in types of identities that can be developed and obstacles that impede how they can be developed.

Identity Development and Agency

Côté (2000) proposed two distinct pathways for agency to function in facilitating identity change: developmental individualization and default individualization.[1] Emerging adults can take the path of **developmental individualization** when agency is high, engaging in the exploration of potential adult roles in search of their identity. Within this pathway, commitment to identities results from extensive exploration and deliberation, leading to thoughtful personal growth. This path of purposeful exploration and reflection leads to an actively built identity and actively formed social bonds and commitments, including the development of a meaningful life or identity project (Côté, 2000, 2015). Thus, emerging adults who embrace this identity process pathway capitalize on their high levels of agency in this developmental phase.

In contrast, emerging adults take the identity process pathway of **default individualization** when agency is low. Within this pathway, they may ignore the opportunity to explore, fail to generate these opportunities or be obstructed from exploration and growth. Without embracing their agentic capabilities, emerging adults are likely left without adequate preparation to make successful commitments to adult roles. This inaction in attempting to make identity changes removes the agentic activity of making decisions and taking action. This "path of least resistance" (Côté, 2015, p. 535) leads to a passively formed identity and passively formed social bonds and commitments (Côté, 2000, 2015).

Interestingly, these two pathways offer a (somewhat) parallel operationalization to the themes encompassed in Maruna's seminal 2001 text "Making Good". In his research, Maruna (2001) found two pathways similar to those of Côté (2000, 2015). The first is that of the **redemption script**, where ex-offenders actively embrace desistance (Maruna, 2001). Through this script, they work toward a "redemption" of their identity whereby they acknowledge past involvement in crime as an opportunity to learn from and facilitate moral growth. This script is similar to the developmental individualization pathway in that young people who engage in role exploration permit themselves an opportunity for personal growth over the life course and maturation over one's younger self. This pathway falls in line with what is expected of emerging adults who are exploring their identity options in society (Marcia, 1966,1980), and who can capitalize on the identity moratorium of emerging adulthood to transition into identity achievement.

The second pathway is that of the **persistent offender**, or an individual who did not think they could successfully desist (Maruna, 2001). Those who fell into this pathway clung to the familiarity of criminal or deviant activity instead of working to break out of this identity, similar to the default individualization pathway presented above. Young people who do not capitalize on, or are unable to capitalize on, scripts for redemptions and maturation may not be as well prepared to fit adult roles into their identity as their peers exercising high levels of agentic activity. This pathway encompasses the experiences of young people who may not or cannot capitalize on exploring their identity options and end up in a phase of identity foreclosure or diffusion (Marcia, 1966, 1980). As a result, they generally accept the roles and identities placed upon them in society, which may mean that those with histories of justice system involvement are stagnant in this identity. The conceptual link between the work of Maruna and Côté demonstrates the role agency can play in the desistance process, and how identity development is embedded in the potential mechanism for desistance.

Agency, however, is not the only factor that contributes to which pathway young people take in their identity maturation and desistance processes. As "people are expected to be the architects of their own destinies" (Côté & Allahar, 2006, p. 115; see also Côté, 2015, p. 535), understanding how external factors may influence the attempts at constructing these "destinies" is imperative. First, as we live in societies comprised of social groups and limited resources, one's position as a social actor in this space matters to the individual. The identity, thus, represents the reputation of the individual both internally and externally in social contexts (McAdams & Zapata-Gietl, 2015; see also Arnett, 2016). Surely, identity and behavior are intimately linked to one another, as there is typically a consistency between the two (Burke & Reitzes, 1981; Paternoster & Bushway, 2009). As a social actor, a person will perform the roles associated with their own self-perception and/or external reputation. How one perceives their own identity can mediate the choices in behavior, including involvement in crime (Rise et al., 2010; Rocque et al., 2016).

Second, the transition to adulthood offers the opportunity to explore various roles and to establish a goal-oriented framework for the future self (McAdams & Zapata-Gietl, 2015). As a result of the delays in turning points indicative of emerging adulthood, traditional markers of adulthood have shifted. The identity formation process across the life course has become more individualized for young people. This individualization is reflected through the efforts of experimenting with and committing to adult roles (Schwartz et al., 2005).

Identity Development in a Social Context

Our identities change as we transition across life stages and take on different social roles (Erikson, 1968; Thoits & Virshup, 1997; Yamaguchi & Kandel, 1985).

As Erikson argued, these identities serve the important purpose of being a bridge between the younger and current self and provide a continuity to the concept of self as a person transitions through the life course (Bamberg, 2011; Kroger & Marcia, 2011). This identity change and development is central to the transition into adulthood (Côté, 2002; Klimstra et al., 2010). Who someone is can change across the life course, and often does as a result of intentional actions (Kiecolt, 1994). Therefore, these identities can be linked to the life stage a person is in, and a change in identity can facilitate the transition across life stages.

Young people often embrace this identity development through the **identity project**. As DeLuca and colleagues described it, the identity project serves as a "virtual bridge between challenging present circumstances and an uncertain, but hoped-for, future" (DeLuca et al., 2016, p. 9). Identity projects are frameworks through which young people can form or change their identities. Typically, these identity projects relate to how one presents themselves to the social world under some principal theme. Young people may, for example, embrace the identity project of becoming a "good college student" or "a best friend" or "a good romantic partner". For emerging adults, identity projects coincide with the transition out of adolescence and into adulthood.

As justice-involved young people age through the life course and embrace desistance, they actively work to make the transition from an antisocial identity into a more prosocial identity (e.g., stopping selling illegal drugs and finding legal employment). These identity projects provide justice-involved young people with a blueprint toward desistance, separating the past self from the future self one hopes to become (DeLuca et al., 2016; Maruna, 2001). Identity projects offer "hooks for change" (Giordano et al., 2002, 2007), working as turning points for justice-involved young adults. To do this, they must employ some agentic activity. This agentic activity is pivotal to embracing identity transformation within the desistance process (King, 2013; Stone, 2016). But social and structural factors, such as relationships, gender, and socioeconomic status, can support or inhibit the efforts of agentic activity one pours into developing their identity.

It is especially important to examine if and how these socio-structural factors of emerging adulthood differentially affect emerging adults with histories of justice system involvement. The context of these socio-structural factors, as discussed in Chapter 1, looks unique for today's emerging adult as it interacts with the agency required of young people to engage in identity development, limiting the availability of social identities and thus the opportunity to transition into a new self. Consequently, understanding how individuals mitigate the social-structural factors or barriers they face is necessary to understand their identity change process (Côté, 2002).

Justice-involved young people face obstacles, or "snares" (Moffitt, 1993), in building their identity projects, such as social (e.g., no professional references for a job application) and structural barriers (e.g., no relevant work experience; criminal record). These barriers include limited prosocial opportunities (Augustyn & McGloin, 2018), interruptions in developmental maturation (Dmitrieva et al., 2012; Rocque et al., 2016; Steinberg, 2009), and discrimination in seeking employment and establishing financial stability (Augustyn & Loughran, 2017; Bottoms & Shapland, 2011; Fader, 2013; Siennick & Widdowson, 2020; Western, 2002). These barriers, or "snares", in the path of desistance may also include traditionally accepted turning points that occur at inopportune moments in the life course, such as becoming a parent at too young of an age or to too many children (Moffitt, 1993; Wojciechowski, 2021).

Additionally, there may be intersectional issues compounding this, as other marginalized societal statuses (e.g., socioeconomic status, race, ethnicity, gender) may contribute to a difficult transition out of crime (Bersani & Doherty, 2018; Lee & Waithaka, 2017). In particular, Black and Latino young people face greater threats to the maturation and desistance processes (Doherty & Ensminger, 2014; Harding & Harris, 2020; Piquero, 2015). Social-structural barriers, thus, must be considered in their interaction with agentic activities within the desistance process. Researchers must conceptualize and operationalize these factors within the same theories and models to appropriately understand the processes of identity development among justice-involved emerging adults. This is especially important when taking into consideration the social inequalities reinforced within justice-involved communities (see Wakefield & Uggen, 2010).

Considering the Challenges of Identity Exploration Among Justice-Involved Populations

While exploring adult social roles and identity projects may be typical of the general emerging adult population, justice-involved emerging adults are often limited in their capacities to fully embrace this period of exploration. The formal label of "criminal" and harsh punishments, including long sentences, inhibit the beginning or continuing of the transition into adulthood and the attaining of traditional adulthood markers (Uggen & Wakefield, 2005; see also Pager, 2003). People with histories of justice system involvement may be hindered in their transition into adulthood because of issues with obtaining employment, their socioeconomic status, struggles with addiction, and challenges to maintaining positive relationships (Healy, 2013). This label is particularly salient for those with criminal records, as employers may be less willing to interview or hire someone with a criminal record (Lindsay, 2022; Pager, 2003; Pager et al., 2009; Uggen et al., 2014). They are also less likely to establish the relationships and behaviors necessary for prosocial adult roles (Uggen et al., 2004).

Generally, emerging adults may thrive on the freedom to explore which is characteristic of this period in the life course. However, this is not always the case.

Many emerging adults will have feelings of uncertainty in themselves and their future, reporting that they feel lost, which may facilitate mental health symptoms or other stressors (Arnett, 2007). They will also face failure, rejection, or disappointment in their exploration across the domains of relationships, employment, and worldviews. Emerging adults may, for example, face rejection or disappointment in their romantic explorations, or failure in their efforts to establish independent housing from their parents. They may also experience failure in attempting to achieve their career goals or find satisfying and fulfilling work. Additionally, in the effort to establish a new worldview, the destruction of the one they were brought up with may not immediately be filled by a new or more amenable alternative (Arnett, 2000; Arnett & Jensen, 2002).

Such implications are especially important for marginalized and vulnerable populations (Lee & Waithaka, 2017), including those involved with the justice system (Arnett, 2007; Osgood et al., 2005). Barriers created by justice-involvement often inhibit the occurrence of or access to traditional markers of adulthood (Abrams & Terry, 2017; Fader, 2013; Harding & Harris, 2020; Uggen et al., 2004; Western, 2006). This creates an opportunity for the negative consequences of identity transformation to be exacerbated for justice-involved emerging adults, impeding their ability to shed their current identity tied to antisocial or criminal behavior to embrace a new identity. Thus, although aging out of crime may be imperative to the transition into adulthood (Uggen & Massoglia, 2003) and prosocial adult roles can be identified that may influence desistance (Uggen & Wakefield, 2008), this discrepancy between current identity and barriers to a future identity may cause some existential confusion and uncertainty for young people trying to desist (Farrall & Calverley, 2006). Maturation, however, may offer an opportunity for young people to engage in identity change and overcome some of these barriers in their processes of desistance (Coyle, 2019).

Maturation

Maturation is a process through which one develops across biological, psychological, and social domains (Glueck & Glueck, 1937, 1940; Rocque, 2015). The concept of maturation in criminology is not new – it started within the work of Sheldon and Eleanor Glueck and their linking of maturation with a mechanism that facilitates a decrease in crime with age. The mechanism of maturation works in that as a young person matures over time, they begin to make decisions or choose more responsible behaviors. Maturation, thus, functions as a process by which young people grow into responsible adults in society, grounded in the attachment to society's prosocial norms – things like avoiding deviance, following the law, getting a job, contributing to the economy, and contributing to society.

The process of maturation is not theorized to necessarily occur naturally with age (Rocque, 2015). Instead, an individual must actively choose (or at least not resist) their own maturation process. Inherently, this process of maturation is both personal and social. In their work on maturation, the Gluecks recognized this, and discussed the importance of maturation across the biological, psychological, and social facets of one's life (Glueck & Glueck, 1937, 1968, 1974). Thus, age and physical development (i.e., **biological maturation**) operationalizes just one component within the maturation triad. **Psychological maturation** includes largely introspective components of maturation, such as self-control, planning for the future, self-respect, and perseverance. This largely centers on how one views themselves, the perceptions of their own identity, or "who they are". Finally, **social maturation** is grounded in one's environmental conditions, personal relationships, work and educational efforts, and recreational activities or hobbies/interests.

The discussion of maturation, its processes, and its place within the life course has been largely critiqued within criminology (e.g., Laub & Sampson, 1991; see also Greenberg, 1977; Sutherland, 1937; Wootton, 1962). However, the works of Rocque (2012, 2015) and colleagues (Rocque et al., 2015, 2016, 2019) have brought maturation back to the forefront of understanding desistance within the life course. Rocque (2015) expands on previous theorization and critiques, proposing five domains of maturation: Civic/Communal Maturation, Psychosocial Maturation, Adult Social Role Maturation, Cognitive Transformation/Identity Maturation, and Neurocognitive Maturation (see Table 2.2).

TABLE 2.2 Domains of Adult Maturation

Domain	*Description/examples*
Neurocognitive Maturation	• Changes in brain structure • Improvement in working memory, intelligence, and executive functioning
Cognitive Transformation & Identity Maturation	• Changes in self-perception • Changes in attitudes toward social institutions and deviance
Psychosocial Maturation	• Perspective: Future orientation, conscientiousness • Responsibility: Independence, autonomy • Temperance: Rationality, self-control, lack of aggression and impulsivity
Adult Social Role Maturation	• Maintaining adult relationships, such as cohabitation or marriage • Employment/career – and satisfaction within it • Becoming a parent
Civic & Communal Maturation	• Being a good citizen to society • Activities such as voting, paying taxes, and communal/volunteer work

Source: Adapted from Rocque (2015, p. 351).

This conceptualization of maturation offers a mechanism to weave together concepts from theories of identity transformation, life course criminology, and emerging adulthood. First, all emerging adults are likely progressing through biological maturation, encompassing Rocque's domain of neurocognitive maturation. Interestingly, the Gluecks mapped the maturation process onto the life course to happen between the ages of 25 and 35 (Glueck & Glueck, 1943), overlapping with the theorization of emerging adulthood (Arnett, 2000, 2015, 2016). They also recognized that young people who could not mature out of deviance in this part of the life course may end up as lifelong, or "career", criminals.

Psychological maturation encompasses Rocque's domains of cognitive transformation/identity maturation and psychosocial maturation. These domains function in line with theories on identity, identity transformation, and agency discussed throughout the chapter (Côté, 2000, 2015; Marcia, 1966, 1980; Maruna, 2001; Schwartz et al., 2005). Understanding that a young person's identities change as they move through the life course (i.e., as they mature), the histories of these changes remain integral to how a young person views themselves (Bamberg, 2011; Kroger & Marcia, 2011). Changes to identity are typically intentional for young people working to mature through the life course (Côté, 2002; Kiecolt, 1994; Klimstra et al., 2010). They hone in on the concepts presented by Rocque (2015), which are perspective, responsibility, and temperance. These in turn facilitate a recognition of psychological maturation within oneself and within one's interactions with society.

Finally, social maturation is captured within adult social role maturation and civic/communal maturation. These two domains encompass the social activities normative for adults engaging in prosocial society, echoing literature from both life course criminology and emerging adulthood (e.g., Berlin et al., 2010; Furstenberg, 2006, 2008, 2010; Furstenberg et al., 2005; Lee & Waithaka, 2017; Settersten & Ray, 2010). Changes to relationships and social roles are typical for young people working to mature through the life course. Often, young people progressing through the life course are actively working to establish new contexts for social relationships and engagements with social institutions.

While maturation is important for all young people to progress through the life course, it may be especially important for young adults who face barriers in achieving other adult roles. Through establishing maturation across these domains, young people who face these barriers have an opportunity to overcome the inaccessibility of some normative adulthood roles (Coyle, 2019; Matza, 1964). This may be imperative for justice-involved emerging adults who cannot access traditional turning points such as getting a college degree, establishing a career, buying a home, or establishing autonomy and independence. Maturation, thus, can offer a mechanism to extend theorizations of identity and desistance into the life course of emerging adults.

Conclusion

Identity change and transformation are an integral part of the transition to adulthood for young people. An individual's identity is their perception of who they are both individually and within the context of society. Young people naturally go through a process of trying to establish their identity as a part of their transition to adulthood. Establishing this identity is important cognitive work within the maturation process for young people, signaling both internally and externally that a young person has matured. Therefore, identity changes serve as a bridge between the younger and the current (or future) self.

Identity development and change are influenced by an individual's level of agency, social conditions, and structural factors. Agency here refers to the active engagement in behaviors that facilitate identity maturation, development, and change. Social and structural factors include those that can support or inhibit the efforts of agentic activity a person engages in, such as relationships, gender, or socioeconomic status. The context of these social and structural factors has changed for emerging adults when compared to previous generations of youth. This, in turn, has influenced how young people activate agency in their processes of identity development and the expectations of the identity development process. Desistance researchers need to further their understanding of identity development and maturation within the context of emerging adulthood in order to refine theory and practice for justice-involved young people.

Ultimately, adult social roles (i.e., turning points or identity projects) provide emerging adults with meaning, fulfillment, and stability. This stage of emerging adulthood offers justice-involved emerging adults the opportunity to experiment with adult social roles and embrace personal growth through exploration and building identity projects (Kroger & Marcia, 2011; McAdams, 2013). Through this exploration, emerging adults will establish ideologies (i.e., values and beliefs), begin a vocation (i.e., how they want to function within an adult economy), and develop relationships (McAdams, 2013). This stage in development affords an opportunity to become the author of an integrative life story that links a reconstructed past, perceived present, and imagined future, providing continuity to the life story (McAdams, 1988; McAdams et al., 1996; see also Erikson, 1968). The perspective toward oneself and one's maturation process may in turn influence future behaviors, identity formation, and social connections to others (Farrall et al., 2011; Healy, 2013; Mizel & Abrams, 2018).

Note

1 Evans and Heinz (1994) offer a comparable conceptualization of active and passive individualization, respectively. I rely more heavily here on Côté's (2000, 2015) work because of its application to emerging adulthood.

3

METHODOLOGICAL APPROACH

Identity Change Through Narratives

In line with the research presented in the first two chapters, young people working through the life course face a great challenge with establishing or changing their identities. As they grow up, adolescents (and now emerging adults) experience a phase of **identity crisis** (Erikson, 1970). As Erikson defines this phase of identity crisis, he discusses how young people engage in both conscious and unconscious efforts of role exploration and conflict within one's identity. This identity crisis percolates during the transition out of adolescence and into adulthood. For a young person to provide continuity between their past younger self and future mature self, they must work to construct their experiences and choices into a coherent narrative to facilitate a sense of identity cohesion.

Identity cohesion across the life course can be achieved through one's work as an autobiographical "author" who can reconstruct the past and build images of the future. One's life story narrative can be successfully internalized and facilitate the development of one's identity (McAdams & Zapata-Gietl, 2015). As "stories give us our identities" (McAdams, 2006a, p. 76), personal narratives are at their essence *the* identity (McAdams, 1988, 1997, 2006b). The question of identity and "Who are you?" can be addressed through a qualitative narrative, which can provide a voice to the identity (Vignoles, 2018) as a narrative allows people to weave together the generally disconnected events of life into a cohesive story (Ricoeur, 1992; Vaughan, 2007). Identity and the process of developing, maintaining, or changing this identity can be presented through the narrative, and in both personal and social contexts (Maruna, 2001; Vignoles, 2018).

DOI: 10.4324/9781003143581-4

Interestingly, Erikson (1970) challenges that this identity crisis happens similarly for all young people. In his discussion of the identity crisis, he acknowledges that while developmental (e.g., physical, cognitive) factors are central to this crisis and progression toward cohesion, social and structural components provide an important context for the opportunities of young people to resolve their identity crises. Erikson argues that the identity crisis a young person experiences is individualized. Some young people experience a crisis that is hardly noticeable, either to themselves or to others. Other young people must experience a very visible and transparent identity crisis in order to progress through their development into adulthood.

Erikson also aptly discusses how social and structural factors play an important role in influencing the experience of the identity crisis for youth. He argues (Erikson, 1970, p. 732):

> The crisis is sometimes hardly noticeable and sometimes very much so: in some young people, in some classes, at some periods in history, the identity crisis will be noiseless; in other people, classes, and periods, the crisis will be clearly marked off as a critical period of 'second birth,' institutionalized by ceremonial procedure, or intensified by collective strife or individual conflict.

This recognition of socio-structural impacts on youth development mimics the arguments presented by DeLuca and colleagues (2016) discussed in the Introduction of this book regarding the applicability of the term *emerging* adulthood. Not all youth have the same opportunities to emerge into adulthood – some may end up on an *expedited* path (DeLuca et al., 2016) or even a *prolonged* path (Salvatore et al., 2012) to an adult self.

Regardless of the expediency of this path, young people remain the autobiographical "author" of their own life stories and personal narratives. Justice-involved emerging adults can still create a coherent adult identity by linking together their status as a social actor and experiences as a motivated agent through the construction of the life story (McAdams & Zapata-Gietl, 2015; Presser & Sandberg, 2015; Schwartz et al., 2005). Creating a positive image for their future self and setting goals for embracing adult roles through the narrative may facilitate the success of desistance (Paternoster & Bushway, 2009). Establishing a goal-oriented future and committing to prosocial roles can support the influence of additional factors in the success of desistance, such as conventional social bonds (Giordano et al., 2002; Vaughan, 2007). Overall, utilizing a narrative methodology allows researchers to move beyond incident-driven understandings of crime that are separate from "the personal or social context" (Vaughan, 2007, p. 402; see also Maruna & Copes, 2005; Presser & Sandberg, 2015). Researchers can instead work to understand how identity may play a role in the desistance from crime and utilize a methodology that can account for the complexity of this relationship (Vaughan, 2007).

Integrating the Narrative Identity and the Identity Status Models

The **narrative identity model** is grounded in the work of McAdams and his interpretations of Erikson's classical theory (see McAdams, 2001; McAdams & Cox, 2010). This model is centered on the content of identity development through the story of how someone has become the person they are through their past memories. Thus, in this model, the personal story is connected to the past through a personal and reflective process (McLean, Syed, & Shucard, 2016; Pasupathi et al., 2007). This process of reflection on the past to make sense of the present self is known as **autobiographical reasoning** (Habermas & Bluck, 2000; Habermas & Köber, 2015). The ability to participate in this method of reasoning is indicative of the transition into adulthood (see McLean et al., 2016a) and is suitable for capturing negative, disruptive, or difficult events (Thorne et al., 2004) including experiences of crime, deviance, justice-system involvement, and victimization (Presser & Sandberg, 2015). This is likely because these events require more effort to comprehend and process (Bruner, 1990; Presser & Sandberg, 2015). Additionally, there are several methods to engage in this autobiographical reasoning, including meaning-making (e.g., McLean & Pratt, 2006; McLean, Syed, Yoder, & Greenhoot, 2016) and making connections across the events of life (e.g., Pasupathi & Mansour, 2006).

The **identity status model**, reviewed in Chapter 2, is centered on the identity process of exploration and commitment. Exploration involves the activities related to actively engaging in finding out "who" someone is, such as dating, talking to others, and exploring vocations. Commitment, then, involves embracing a specific pathway toward defining the "who". This transition from exploration to commitment is progressive and gradual across the life course for young people (Kroger et al., 2010; Schwartz, 2001).

To understand identity development, both the content and processes must be understood. Using an integrated model that applies narrative methods to study the content and the identity status model to study the processes has been recommended for identity researchers (see McLean, Syed, & Shucard, 2016). Previous research has found that using an integrated model has helped to elucidate how identity processes vary across content types (see McLean, Syed, & Shucard, 2016; McLean, Syed, Yoder, & Greenhoot, 2016). Thus, this research by McLean and colleagues concludes that different identity contents require different types of processing. Researchers, and criminologists in particular, must therefore work to expand the understanding of identity development within criminology to understand the content and processes related to embracing identities of desistance. Narrative methodologies coupled with the study of identity change and status offer the opportunity to do just this (McLean, Syed, & Shucard, 2016; McLean, Syed, Yoder, & Greenhoot, 2016; Presser & Sandberg, 2015)

The Methodological Approach to Data Collection and Analysis

Given this context around the identity crisis, identity change, and identity cohesion, my focus in this research is to explore how young people can make the transition into adulthood within their own stories of desistance. The focus of the subsequent chapters and data presented in this book are grounded in the following research question:

> *What turning points do emerging adults identify as important to the desistance process and their identity transformation into prosocial adulthood?*

Throughout this book, I will draw on evidence from qualitative interviews conducted with young adults engaged in the desistance process, integrating interdisciplinary research and theory across the fields of criminology and sociology, developmental psychology, and emerging adulthood. Before I outline the methodology of this analysis, it is important to discuss how this data was collected.

Recruitment

To recruit participants for this project, I worked alongside a community-based intervention program (herein, the community-based program) in the Northeastern part of the United States. This community-based program focused on serving youth and young adults formally engaged in the criminal justice system. Almost all of the young people involved in the program either had a felony conviction, were in the process of reentry from prison or jail, or were involved with a local gang.

Participants in the community-based program had access to an array of services, including employment, education, and case managers to assist with the justice system. Importantly though, this program was entirely voluntary. Young people who engaged in the program chose to do so of their own volition. I purposefully sought out this population for this study in order to understand what their processes of desistance entailed. This allowed me to explore what components these young people considered as motivators in the desistance process, in an effort to help me build and refine theory around accessing turning points for justice-involved emerging adults. This included allowing participants to define what they consider to be turning points, and how they access these turning points, as well as what they do when they cannot access these or other turning points typical for their age group.

To facilitate recruitment and familiarity with potential participants, I spent approximately one year engaging with the community-based organization prior to beginning study recruitment. This process began with meeting with staff and leaders in the organization to understand the function and mission of the organization, as well as gain institutional knowledge of the program and services offered. I also often asked staff members and volunteers questions to gain insight into the experiences of the young people they work with and identify concepts to include in my qualitative interview protocol. In addition, I worked with the organization's staff to identify questions they were interested in having answered by empirical data, ultimately conducting a quantitative analysis of the organization's participant records to help them understand retention in programming. I merged these findings with the qualitative findings at the end of the project to provide context to these results in a formal report the organization could utilize in seeking grant funding and other resources.

Prior to initiating study recruitment, I spent a few months participating in the activities and programs hosted by the program. I worked alongside young people in their job placements, attended group check-ins and meetings, joined the young people and staff during their lunch hour, hung around the facilities in designated leisure spaces, and attended special events hosted by the organization such as performances, talent shows, volunteer activities, and sporting events. During this process, I began to introduce the project to young people and explain my role as a researcher in trying to understand their experiences and the impact their stories would have on the field. The young people came to know that I was working independently of the community-based organization, as I was never assigned an office space or made decisions about their job placements or evaluated their performance.

The majority of participants were recruited through this on-site recruitment strategy. They came up to me while I was on the premises and asked for more information about the study and to schedule a time for an interview. There were a few participants later in the sample who were influenced through snowball sampling from previous participants.

Sample

Participants were purposefully recruited for this study, as the goal of this research is to understand the desistance process for justice-involved emerging adults and contextualize the findings of this research to present avenues for

TABLE 3.1 List of Participants and Pseudonyms

Pseudonym	*Age*	*Gender*	*Race/Ethnicity*
Bruno	25	Male	Latino
Carlos	21	Male	Latino
Daniel	18	Male	Latino
Diego	22	Male	Latino
Dylan	22	Male	White
Emma	22	Female	Multiracial
Kareem	22	Male	Multiracial
Lucas	18	Male	Latino
Mateo	18	Male	Latino
Sebastian	24	Male	Multiracial
Sean	21	Male	Multiracial
Selena	21	Female	Latino
Steve	25	Male	White
Tiffany	25	Female	Other
Zoe	22	Female	White

future research. Fifteen emerging adults between the ages of 18 and 25 were recruited and interviewed as a part of this study. Table 3.1 provides a list of the participants' pseudonyms as well as some basic demographic characteristics. All of the participants had a history of justice system involvement, including gang involvement, arrest, and/or incarceration. On average, participants were about 22 years old and had spent around a year involved with the community-based organization actively engaging in their own desistance processes.

Interview Protocol

A narrative methodological approach was used to collect interview data on life histories, including significant experiences and events (Creswell, 2007). Through narratives, participants can engage in authoring an integrative story linking reflections of their past with their present and creating a vision for the future (Erikson, 1968; McAdams, 1988; McAdams et al., 1996). I used a semi-structured Life Story Interviews (LSI) protocol to facilitate the construction of a narrative through significant life moments (McAdams, 2008). Through the interviews, participants were able to present their life stories which provided the greatest possible context to their experiences with identity transformation, building social bonds and relationships, and embracing desistance. The LSI used for this study is a modified version of the original template created by McAdams (1993, 2008). Modifications to the LSI are common among researchers interested in capturing specific life experiences

TABLE 3.2 Life Story Interview (LSI)

LSI Section	*Questions/Items*
Key Scenes	• High Point • Low Point • Turning Point • Positive Childhood Memory • Negative Childhood Memory Wisdom Event
Future	• The "Next Chapter" in your story • Dreams, hopes, and plans for the future • Life Project
Challenges Faced	• What were the challenges? • Were challenges overcome? If so, how?
Life Theme	• Description of theme to overall narrative/story

(see Adler et al., 2017). The adapted LSI items used for this study are included in Tables 3.2 and 3.3.

Table 3.2 presents the classical components of the LSI utilized in this study (McAdams, 2008; see also Adler et al., 2017). The focus of these questions was to allow participants to identify key points they felt were important in their life story, their transition into adulthood, and their desistance processes. I began each interview by explaining to participants why the interview was structured in this fashion in order to prompt them to think reflectively about their own experiences. The goal of this section of the interview was to identify key events in each participant's narratives of identity transformation and development into adulthood.

Participants were asked to identify and describe important events in their own "stories" such as a high point, low point, turning point from a low into high point, positive and negative childhood memories, and a time when they demonstrated wisdom in their actions or an event where they were proud of

TABLE 3.3 Life Story Interview Supplement

LSI Section	*Questions/Items*
Community	What does community mean to you? How would you define your community? How do you feel about being a part of your community? What are your experiences in your community? Where did you learn to be a part of a community? What does a "good" community member do?
Relationships	What are your most important relationships? How do you feel about your relationships with these people? What is so important about these relationships? Where did you learn how to be a part of these relationships?

their own behavior. Then, I asked participants about the future they see for their narrative, including the next "chapter" in their story, a project they wanted to work toward across their life, and their dream, hopes, and plans for the future. I also asked participants to identify challenges they faced in their life as well as if they saw any themes as being important for their story or character development.

Table 3.3 presents the supplemental questions participants were asked about their experiences with their communities and their relationships. The goal of this section was to identify social and structural components which may influence how young people develop their identity and desist within their maturation into adulthood. These questions were informed by evidence from the existing literature as well as by other research studies that have adapted the LSI for similar populations (e.g., McAdams et al., 1996; McCabe & Dinh, 2018) and recommendations proposed by narrative experts (Adler et al., 2017).

Additional questions were asked of participants relating to their experiences with the community-based organization that were used to assist in the understanding of retention in programming. As the study in this text is not a program evaluation, these questions are not listed to help protect the privacy of the program, and ultimately of the participants in this study.

Analytic Approach

In approaching the data coding and analysis in this work, I drew from a grounded theory methodology. Traditionally, grounded theory is defined by three main components: immersion in the research field, sampling toward theoretical saturation, and inductive analytic coding (Glaser & Strauss, 1967). First, as described earlier in this chapter, I engaged in immersion in the research field prior to and during my recruitment process with the community-based program. Additionally, I sampled toward a theoretical saturation by collecting, coding, and analyzing the data from participant interviews, identifying persistent and emerging themes, and then returning to the research field to collect more data through new interviews.

To facilitate sampling toward theoretical saturation, I followed the constant comparative method to facilitate the validity of the coding schemes (Glaser & Strauss, 1967). The constant comparative method combines systematic data collection, coding, and analysis with theoretical sampling for the purpose of theme and theory generation (Conrad et al., 1993; Glaser, 1965; Glaser & Strauss, 1967; Kolb, 2012). An initial coding scheme was developed after the first five interviews using open coding techniques with the data, including comparing data across participants, conceptualizing codes, and then categorizing data (Strauss & Corbin, 1998). This coding scheme was informed by the existing literature on the topic areas of interest for this study while allowing for new themes to emerge in the coding process. This included coding the data for themes of turning points, maturation, and desistance.

After this initial coding, I refined the coding scheme to create axial codes to validate the relationships among the data. This axial coding process allowed central themes to be broken down into more specific categories and concepts (Strauss & Corbin, 1998), such as the types of turning points or the types and quality of relationships. Following this, I engaged in additional participant recruitment to test the axial coding scheme developed from initial interviews and integrate new findings until reaching a point of saturation for the data (Strauss & Corbin, 1998). As new evidence was added to a code, I re-examined that code for new commonalities and divergences, adjusting the coding schema as I went. In doing this, I sought out additional participants who allowed me to refine the coding scheme I developed as well as provided the opportunity to gain new insights (Strauss & Corbin, 1998; Taylor et al., 2015).

Finally, my coding process applied "theoretical" thematic analysis (Braun & Clarke, 2006) as I drew from previously existing themes in the research from life course criminology and developmental psychology. Additionally, I used an abductive coding technique (Timmermans & Tavory, 2012; also Deterding & Waters, 2018) in place of a true inductive coding process. Abductive coding acknowledges that research may not be truly inductive as a result of exposure to previous research, knowledge, and theory. However, it still calls for analysis that is open to unexpected or divergent findings (Timmermans & Tavory, 2012). Therefore, although this study draws from a grounded theory approach, a true grounded theory approach in the vein of Glaser and Strauss (1967) is not applied here.

Agency Among Participants

Participants in this study all fall into the agentic pathway of developmental individualization discussed in Chapter 2. The participants recognized that they were in the process of exploring various adult roles and actively working toward establishing themselves within these prosocial roles and identities. In line with the work of Côté (2000, 2015) and Maruna (2001), the desistance narratives of this population attempted to balance the connection between negative past experiences or behaviors with present and future identities. As these participants were actively working on exploring their identity options, they also fell into categories of identity achievement and identity moratorium (Marcia, 1966, 1980) in different facets of their lives. While they were generally able to "hook" onto change and desistance (Giordano et al., 2002) through this exploration, many of the participants also faced barriers in some facets of identity exploration.

As evidence throughout this text will demonstrate how they embrace identity exploration, it will also highlight domains under which identity exploration is low, indicative of Marcia's (1966, 1980) identity foreclosure and identity diffusion statuses.

Participants commonly expressed that they were in the process of trying to "get on track", as phrased by Lucas, and that this was pivotal to their desistance process. The participants were trying to reduce their engagement in antisocial or deviant behaviors and cut ties with networks that facilitate their engagement in these activities. By getting "on track", participants refer to getting back to behaviors, roles, and relationships that are more prosocial in nature. For them, this return to a prosocial life reflects a return to their "real" identity in their narrative (see Maruna, 2001; Presser, 2004).

Throughout the evidence presented in the subsequent chapters, I work to identify areas where the justice-involved emerging adults in this sample achieved success and faced challenges in their own attempts at maturation and desistance. My goal in this effort is to recognize and codify these successes and challenges to help facilitate both a better understanding of the context of findings in this study as well as inform (or at least encourage other researchers to explore how) success and challenges affect an emergence into prosocial adulthood.

4

IDENTITY AND PSYCHOLOGICAL MATURATION

As young people progress through the life course, they face a great deal of instability as they work to identify who they are and what their role is in society. Young people spend this phase of the life course after adolescence testing out various roles and paths they could take for their futures. This exploration of the possibilities of who one can be when they grow up is integral to the process of transitioning into an adult (Erikson, 1950, 1968; Keniston, 1971; Levinson, 1986). Instability, thus, is one of the defining features of this stage in the life course (Arnett, 2000). This lack of stability is accepted and even expected for young people as they embrace the opportunities to explore new roles, challenges, and relationships.

Under emerging adulthood theory, as young people establish stability across some facets of their identity, this can serve to signify a transition into adulthood. As they ascertain permanent roles within the components of life (i.e., romantic relationships, career, housing, financial security), this can facilitate stability within each of these contexts. For example, when a young person finds a long-term romantic partner, they may establish a sense of finality in that aspect of their identity. However, they can still experiment in other aspects of their adult identity, such as in their career, among friends and family, or in their worldviews.

Interestingly, this conceptualization under emerging adulthood theory mirrors much of the discussion surrounding maturation with criminology. The idea of maturation in criminology began within the works of Sheldon and Eleanor Glueck (e.g., 1937, 1940, 1943, 1968) theorizing maturation as the mechanism which facilitates a decrease in crime as people get older. As young people grow up, they begin to embrace the components of maturity and choose behaviors that are more normative for adults, such as getting a job, following laws, and building a family. For maturation to have this effect,

DOI: 10.4324/9781003143581-5

an individual must actively choose, or at least not resist, their own maturation processes across biological, psychological, and social domains (Cauffman & Steinberg, 2000; Glueck & Glueck, 1937, 1968, 1974; Rocque, 2015).

In this and the subsequent chapters, I focus my research on the domains of psychological and social maturation. **Psychological maturation** includes the introspective components of maturation, such as self-control, planning for the future, self-respect, and perseverance. This largely centers on how one views themselves through the perceptions of their own identity or "who they are". **Social maturation** is grounded in one's environmental conditions, personal relationships, work and educational efforts, and recreational activities or hobbies/interests. Much of the literature considers maturation to be a psychosocial process or one that involves components from both psychological and social domains (e.g., Cauffman & Steinberg, 2000; Greenberger & Sørenson, 1964; Steinberg & Cauffman, 1996; Steinberg & Schwartz, 2000).

Maturation and Desistance

The Gluecks originally mapped the maturation process onto the life course between the ages of 25 and 35 (Glueck & Glueck, 1943), roughly in line with current theorizations of emerging adulthood. Criminologists, developmental psychologists, and scholars of desistance have continued to both theorize and find empirical evidence of this relationship between maturation and desistance. In particular, the processes of psychological and social maturation provide a mechanism through which risky behaviors can be reduced and desistance can be accessed (Cauffman & Steinberg, 2000; Monahan et al., 2009; Rocque et al., 2016). The Gluecks (1943) recognized that young people who could not mature out of deviance in this part of the life course may end up as lifelong, or "career", criminals.

Young people involved in the justice system may face increased barriers to achieving maturation (Coyle, 2019; Dmitrieva et al., 2012). In particular, youth who spend time incarcerated may face limits in their ability to engage in activities indicative of maturation that young people typically can engage in on the outside (Dmitrieva et al., 2012; Shulman & Cauffman, 2011). Young people with criminal records may experience disenfranchisement in their reentry process, which can inhibit their access to turning points into prosocial maturation (Manza & Uggen, 2004, 2008; Uggen & Manza, 2005). These effects of justice-system involvement limit the opportunity for young people to practice and establish more mature behaviors.

Consider, for instance, the maturity gap proposed by Moffitt (1993) in the life course. Young people under the adolescent-limited deviance path will desist when they can embrace social and/or psychological maturity. If youth face barriers in doing this, they may end up in a prolonged phase of deviance or even end up in a transition into the life-course-persistent path. The instability of emerging adulthood and the socio-structural shifts affecting access to turning points threatens the desistance of youth on the adolescent-limited deviance path (Salvatore & Taniguchi, 2012; Salvatore et al., 2012). Justice-system involvement and the barriers associated with it may further threaten the natural desistance of youth across the life course. If youth are behind their peers in the maturation process prior to incarceration, then incarceration will only further exacerbate the barriers they face in achieving maturity on pace with their peers in the life course (Monahan et al., 2013). When these youth are released from incarceration and reenter society, they may in turn be more likely to re-engage in deviance (Loughran et al., 2009).

Historically, the Glueck's theories of maturation, their processes, and their place within life course criminology have largely been critiqued (e.g., Wootton, 1962; see also Greenberg, 1977; Laub & Sampson, 1991; Shover, 1985; Sutherland, 1937). However, the work of Rocque (2012, 2015) and colleagues (Rocque et al., 2015, 2016, 2019) has brought maturation back to the forefront of understanding desistance within the life course among criminologists. This perspective toward maturation encompasses much of the empirical work within developmental psychology, providing an interdisciplinary approach expanding the work of the Gluecks and addressing many of the criticisms of maturation posed by life course criminologists.

Rocque (2015) proposes five domains of maturation: Adult Social Role Maturation, Civic/Communal Maturation, Cognitive Transformation/Identity Maturation, Neurocognitive Maturation, and Psychosocial Maturation (see Table 4.1).

TABLE 4.1 Domains of Adult Maturation

Domain	*Description/examples*
Neurocognitive Maturation	• Changes in brain structure • Improvement in working memory, intelligence, and executive functioning
Cognitive Transformation & Identity Maturation	• Changes in self-perception • Changes in attitudes toward social institutions and deviance
Psychosocial Maturation	• Perspective: Future orientation, conscientiousness • Responsibility: Independence, autonomy • Temperance: Rationality, self-control, lack of aggression and impulsivity
Adult Social Role Maturation	• Maintaining adult relationships, such as cohabitation or marriage • Employment/career – and satisfaction within it • Becoming a parent
Civic & Communal Maturation	• Being a good citizen to society • Activities such as voting, paying taxes, and communal/volunteer work

Source: Adapted from Rocque (2015, p. 351).

Young people can engage in the maturation process within each of these domains, whose effects together facilitate the maturation into adulthood.

Rocque's conceptualization of maturation and its domains offers a convenient mechanism through which to translate emerging adulthood theory into the literature on desistance within the life course. In this chapter, I will review the domains of psychological maturation set forth by Rocque. Chapters 5 and 6 will then focus on social maturation across categories of relationships and involvement in society (i.e., employment, civic engagement) respectively. I must also acknowledge here that I exclude the biological domain, neurocognitive maturation, from this text only because I did not target this domain within my data collection, and not because of the importance of this domain. Thus, a limitation of this work is its focus on only the domains of maturation within the social sciences (psychological and social) and its exclusion of the biological domain of maturation.

Cognitive Transformation and Identity Maturation

How a person views themselves, and how they view growth over their own life course provides stability in the face of changes they experience while growing up. As discussed in Chapter 2, identity changes are an integral part of the transition to adulthood for emerging adults (Arnett, 2000; Côté, 2000; Schwartz et al., 2005). The identity change that is central to the transition to adulthood (Côté, 2002; Klimstra et al., 2010) facilitates an opportunity for young people engaged in delinquency to desist under the theorizations of maturation. Participants in this study indeed recognized that they were in the process of exploring various adult roles and actively working toward establishing themselves within these prosocial roles and identities.

Importantly, these young people emphasized that changes in their self-perceptions and attitudes toward deviance had shifted. In line with the work of Côté (2000, 2015) and Maruna (2001), the desistance narratives of participants attempted to balance the connection between negative past experiences or behaviors with present and future identities. Often, they emphasized their engagement in an **identity project** as central to their desistance process. Identity projects provided these young people with "hooks" for change, where they could follow a path toward maturation that allowed them to legitimize this process (Giordano et al., 2002; Maruna, 2001).

While the context of these identity projects looked different for each participant, they provided a route for young people to "get on track", as phrased by Lucas, with their lives. This "track" is one where participants are trying to align with the social and cultural expectations of young people in their community. Largely this track is one of prosocial behavior, where these justice-involved young people were trying to reduce their engagement in antisocial or deviant behaviors and cut ties with networks that facilitate their engagement in these activities. This shift in their self-perceptions as well as their attitudes toward following the law were pivotal to their desistance process. For them, this turn (or return) to a prosocial life reflects their "real" identity within their life story narrative (see Maruna, 2001; Presser, 2004).

Often, participants were able to embrace these "real" identities that they felt were "on track" for their lives through turning points. By having these "hooks for change" (Giordano et al., 2002), participants were able to latch onto an identity they felt was more responsible or worth keeping them out of deviance. Zoe, for example, acknowledges how becoming a mother provided her a path toward desistance:

> I feel like I would have had more room to make bad decisions. I probably would have ... I feel like the only reason why I grew up out of all that negative stuff... like getting expelled and all that, I feel like it would have went further on. Because I even ended up in juvie for like 10 days at one point, and I feel like I probably would have been in [prison] right now for all I know, because I would have had so much freedom. I would have never had any responsibilities

By becoming a mother, Zoe felt she had a "hook" to facilitate change – a "script" for her own redemption narrative. Participants like Zoe accepted their past involvements in criminal or risky behaviors while embracing the opportunity to engage in desistance by establishing new prosocial identities common to adulthood like being a parent.

Acknowledging that they were growing up and maturing played a central role in facilitating the identity shift indicative of the redemption script (Maruna, 2001) among participants. One common tool they used in their narratives was distinguishing their current self from their past self as kids or juveniles. Even at just 18, Lucas emphasizes that he has grown out of being what he terms "hardheaded" – in that he never took anyone's advice when they warned him about getting involved with drug use:

Lucas: ...a lot of people warned me about the life I went into. It went out one ear and into the other.

Interviewer: Do you feel like you've kind of grown out of that at all?

Lucas: Yes, I have. I'm maturer. They can ask me like, "Oh you want this [drug] or that [drug]?" I go like, "Are you stupid?" Like, I'm not a little kid no more. I know what's right or wrong.

As Lucas describes here, ignoring the advice of others, and engaging in drug use, was something that he did when he was not mature. Now, he sees listening to this advice, and avoiding engagement in drug use, as an important part of his maturity. Lucas feels he can distinguish that he's "not a little kid" anymore and that this is his past self. Now, he knows "what's right or wrong", indicating a shift in his attitudes toward deviance and drug use, and a new willingness to follow the law.

Diego, at 22, uses similar language to distinguish his younger, more immature self from who he is today in his emergence into adulthood. He emphasizes this by saying one of his key life chapters occurred when he "was young. [He] was 17 turning 18. [He] was still in high school". Although only 4 or so years ago, Diego marks a shift in his own identity by separating this past self from his current adulthood. This distinction between the past, immature self and the current, more mature (but not necessarily completely mature) self allows these youth to embrace an identity shift within their desistance and redemption narratives.

Importantly, the participants also recognized that developing maturity was a gradual process, and not one that happens immediately or overnight. As Sebastian expresses here, he believed that he was mature when he was 22, but now at 25, reflects that he was not as mature as he believed himself to be at that age:

> I felt like, when I was 22, after I had my first daughter, then [my partner] was like, "I'm pregnant again, four months." I was like, "Oh, shit." I felt, at that point in time, you couldn't tell me nothing… with my [first] daughter, I felt like I had it. I wasn't self-destructing as easy, but I still would. If you keep pushing me, keep pushing me. I used to bottle things up. Now I'm not bottling things up. If I feel some certain way, I'll express it right then and there. I'll call it out right then and there. This is what you're doing, or whatever. I'm not going to just wait, wait, wait, and then explode on you like, "Oh, what the hell was all that for?" Feel me? That's the type of things I used to do.

Here, Sebastian acknowledges that he had achieved some maturity at the age of 22 through exercising self-control (i.e., not self-destructing). Through his interactions and experiences since this time, Sebastian believes that he has more work to do in developing the level of maturity he desires for his adult self. Thus, Sebastian feels he now understands that this process of maturity is gradual and even though he has clear markers for progress in maturing, he recognizes that he has additional development left in his process.

Like many of the other participants, Sebastian also reflected on the importance of listening to others and his ability to accept feedback:

> I'm hearing you, but I'm not listening to you. I can hear you all day. You can speak to me all day, but am I really listening to you? Am I really taking the feedback and pushing it? Pushing it out. You feel me? Like taking it in… in consideration, you feel me?

Sebastian expresses that his "hearing" but "not listening" was indicative of how his previous belief of maturity at 22 was not as well developed as his current definition of maturity at 25. Listening to the advice of others was an important part of maturity for these participants, as emphasized by Sebastian and Lucas earlier. This is in line with research that examines the importance of listening and accepting advice across the life course which indicates that emerging adults may be more likely to accept advice than others in younger developmental stages, especially when they perceive that they have autonomy in taking advice (Carlson, 2014; Liang et al., 2008).

Overall, separating their younger selves and the actions of their younger selves from their current and/or future selves marked an important distinction of maturity for these participants. Maturing allowed these emerging adults to accept their past behaviors while recognizing a shift in their own view of who they are. For justice-involved emerging adults, growing up fits into the "redemption script" (Maruna, 2001), allowing them to accept their past behaviors and work toward establishing a new and more mature self. Recognizing that one is growing up, therefore, provides a mechanism through which emerging adults can shift their identity while providing continuity to their self-perceptions across the life course.

Psychosocial Maturation

Psychosocial maturity is a complex domain within developmental psychology, whose objective is to conceptualize a person's adaptive functioning and socioemotional competence (Galambos & Costigan, 2003; Galambos et al., 2005; Greenberger et al., 1975; Greenberger & Sørenson, 1974). Maturation under this domain largely focuses on development within aspects such as autonomy, interpersonal skills, and social responsibility (Galambos & Costigan, 2003). Three domains are classically codified as an important part of the psychosocial maturation process: temperance, responsibility, and perspective (Steinberg & Cauffman, 1996).

Participants' desistance narratives largely utilized concepts of psychosocial maturity to connect the behaviors of their past (i.e., younger) selves with their current or future (i.e., older) selves. As they are "growing up", these participants believe that they are in control of their own decisions and behaviors, and thus responsible for their outcomes. They recognized that their current and future selves must engage in behavior that is indicative of adulthood, and distinct from the past behaviors of their younger and immature selves. For young people, this psychosocial maturation is an integral part of development and identity change that continues into emerging adulthood (Monahan et al., 2009, 2013).

Diego, for example, expresses this when discussing how he no longer succumbs to pressure from his peers to engage in deviant behavior, "I'm not a little kid, I'm a grown ass man, I do grown ass man shit, you feel me, nobody can tell me what I can and can't do". Here, Diego emphasizes how he plays a role in owning his own maturation and taking accountability for his own actions. Importantly, this also reflects the *social* nature of psychosocial maturation, as Diego emphasizes how he holds himself accountable for being mature in the context of his peers. These domains of psychosocial maturity – temperance, responsibility, and perspective – do not exist as just evidence of cognitive maturity but as the application of this maturity within the context of these young adults' lives and social settings (Modecki, 2008; Steinberg & Cauffman, 1996).

Temperance

First, **temperance** represents the ability to limit behaviors of impulsivity or aggression, transitioning instead to rational decision-making and self-control as influencers of behavior (Steinberg & Cauffman, 1996; see also Gottfredson & Hirschi, 1990). This is especially important for young people with histories of justice-system involvement, who may be subject to harsher punishments for impulsive or aggressive behaviors when compared to their peers without criminal records. Participants in this study identified that being able to exhibit self-control, specifically in regard to their emotions and reactions, was an important aspect of developing their maturity. For example, Daniel identified that changes in his mentality have influenced his behavior:

Daniel: I'm 18 now. I'm going to be 19. I'm still kinda young. Two years ago I had a way different mentality than the mentality I have now. I think if I had my mentality that I have now back then, I [would] be in a way better predicament.

Interviewer: What is it about your mentality that's changed?

Daniel: I handle stuff ... The way I handle myself. If somebody looks at me wrong back then, I would go crazy. But now I don't even pay mind to that.

Similarly, Mateo describes a change in his patterns of thinking and how this influences his behavior. He acknowledges that when he thinks through things before acting, he can limit any impulsive responses. When asked to identify a scene in his story where he displayed wisdom, Mateo said:

> Something wise... like every time I got caught, I would be smarter with it. Every time I got locked up I would think like, this ain't for me. I gotta start changing my life. That's when I maybe started to be smarter. When I did stuff, I didn't think. I was impulsive. When I started using my brain, and think about stuff, I'd calm down and think about it, just stop doing dumb things.

Both Daniel and Mateo attribute changes in their mentality to their maturity, directly linking this to their own behaviors. By thinking about their actions and exhibiting some self-control in their actions, they are both able to limit undesirable consequences.

Several other participants also recognized that by maturing within this domain of temperance they were able to limit negative outcomes, like further involvement in crime or violence. Sean, for example, discusses how he displayed wise decision-making by listening to his conscience on a night when he was around peers who were fighting:

> Just 'cause my conscience was like … I don't know. I don't know how to say it. My ears was telling me something, but my conscience was like, "Naw, it can't be. It don't make sense." If I didn't go off that conscience, if I didn't go off what my conscience was telling me, then I probably would be booked right now. It was a crazy situation, too many people. It was an uncalled for situation. Dudes was fighting, whatever, and dude just did some in-the-way stuff that he needed to do, and that almost caused somebody else to get hurt. If I didn't go with my gut feeling that would've been an even worse night. That'd be the worst, when innocent people get hit or shit happen to innocent people.

Sean, with the assistance of his conscience, recognizes several things here that he thinks he would not have recognized when he was younger and less mature. He acknowledges that getting involved in the fight does not make sense. He postulates that if he did get involved, he could be arrested or could hurt someone innocent. For Sean, this is evidence of his own maturity within the domain of temperance. When asked about how he came to this realization that he should listen to his conscience, Sean said:

> Every time I would just get mad and react, nothing good happened, it'd be a bad outcome. The times I think about like, "All right, let me actually think. Let me relax for a little bit." Shit just played out smooth, letting shit happen. And then at the end of it, you'd be like, "Damn, yeah, that shit wouldnt've been worth it." You feel me? But sometimes you just be mad, you be blackout, you just react off of emotions and then the next day you're like, "Damn, I wish I didn't …" You feel me? If you would've just thought, like, just take 10 seconds to just think, breathe, walk away …

Through his own experiences, Sean was able to learn that by engaging in acts of temperance, such as limiting his aggression and impulsivity and thinking through the potential consequences of his actions, he was experiencing more desirable outcomes. This, for Sean, was central to the recognition of his own interest in and ability to embrace desistance.

Importantly, young people can gradually engage in activities of temperance. Steve, for example, discusses how he engaged in self-control and restraint in his own drug use while he was simultaneously on the run from law enforcement. Steve, who was 25 at the time of his interview, had been involved with the justice system since he was 18, largely for his use of drugs and crimes he committed while under the influence or in an effort to buy/secure illicit substances. During this incident, Steve was not using substances, was on probation, and was on an ankle monitor:

> Yeah. I was actually clean, too, but I was on a bracelet and then I took a plea deal with the judge. My lawyer was like, "You should get it. You've been doing good. Blah blah blah." And the judge didn't accept it and wanted to give me six months. This, that. I panicked. I was mad and I went outside, talked to my lawyer and I ended up just leaving. I cut my bracelet off and then I was on the run.

Here, Steve discusses his (and his lawyer's) belief that he could strike a plea deal to avoid incarceration. When the judge did not accept the plea deal as expected, Steve panicked, acted impulsively, and went "on the run". Steve discusses how while "on the run" and trying to avoid incarceration, he forced himself to stay clean. This choice of sobriety allowed him to keep a clear mind and eventually he was able to rationalize that turning himself in would be the wisest choice:

***Steve*:** But I usually will go on the run and I'll use. I won't care. I stayed clean though. I was on the run still but stayed clean. For maybe almost two weeks I was on the run and then I just went and turned myself in.

***Interviewer*:** And how do you feel, looking back, about that experience and going on the run but then turning yourself in? How do you feel about that?

***Steve*:** I'm surprised that I did it. It just worked out for the better. I could have stayed longer. Then, eventually, maybe I would have got high or something or something could have happened. Catch a new case. Might not be here right now.

Though Steve had made an impulsive and deviant choice in removing his ankle monitor and trying to escape incarceration, he remained cognizant of his need to refrain from drug use. This provides evidence for the possibility of young people to engage in differential applications of self-control as they gradually progress through their maturation processes.

In conducting this interview, I asked Steve why he had made the decision to turn himself in, and he said "I didn't want to die. I literally was scared".

Steve was worried about his own capability to stay clean while on the run, and the consequences if he could not. Steve's father had passed away from an overdose some years earlier. More recently, his cousin passed away from using drugs laced with fentanyl, which prompted his permanent decision to stop using drugs. These tragic losses marked an important part of Steve's experiences and narrative, emphasizing that while an individual must engage in acts of self-control and temperance, these acts do not happen within the vacuum of the individual. Acts of temperance and self-control are influenced by our social contexts and experiences, emphasizing the *social* nature of the psychosocial maturation domain.

Responsibility

The second domain of **responsibility** represents the autonomy of a young person, including their ability to function independently from others (Steinberg & Cauffman, 1996; see also Gottfredson & Hirschi, 1990). Emerging adults often work to establish responsibility through their commitment to identity projects, such as building a family, establishing a career, or civic engagement. For young people, autonomy from parents or family is particularly important, including the ability to establish independent housing and financial stability. Achieving this autonomy, while typical for many emerging adults, may be especially disrupted by justice-system involvement for emerging adults from lower socio-economic classes, who may not have access to generational wealth, parental support, or a family home to live in (Abrams & Terry, 2017; Harding & Harris, 2020). Most of the participants in this study identified financial independence and stability as an important turning point for becoming responsible. Being able to afford to pay their bills or purchase things they want signifies a valuable part of how these participants view their adult self (Arnett, 1998, 2006; Tanner & Arnett, 2009). Financial legitimacy and "clean money", as termed by Sean, are central for the next phase of the life course for these young people as it marks the shift into desistance.

Zoe highlights the importance of financial stability for her own maturation, placing it within the context of her experiences with financial instability and decision-making she considered to be less indicative of this domain of responsibility.

> So this summer I quit a good job I had, because I don't know, I guess I was in a good point at that point. I thought a new job would come. It was a far commute, so I was like, "I'm done with that." It was a stressful ... I didn't really like the job, either. But shortly after, I couldn't find a job that I wanted. I didn't want to work at [a fast food restaurant] or anything like that. So I couldn't find a job. I ended up losing my car, because I couldn't

> pay my insurance, then the registration went, and everything was going downhill, literally, until recently when I came to [the community-based organization]. I started working. It worked out on my schedule. I was able to save money. And now I have my car back on the road. I have my own apartment. Everything's going good. So that's the turning point for me.

For her, saving money, paying for her car insurance, and establishing secure and independent housing were indicative of her turning point into being a responsible adult.

Similarly, as Daniel expresses here, establishing financial security is imperative, stating:

> For me I just want to get my money together. I want to be a better person. I don't want to be in the streets, and having no money, can't do nothing with myself, with the wrong crowd.

Financial security is an important marker for many of these young people's self-perceptions of responsible adulthood. Importantly, Daniel here places this responsibility within his social context. He recognizes that he must achieve this adulthood marker alongside avoiding "the streets" and deviant peers. This self-perception of responsibility is reinforced in the desistance narrative when it is also translated into a young person's social context.

Participants acknowledge the difficulty of embracing this type of independence, where they work to establish financial stability and responsibility. To embrace adulthood, emerging adults often accept the struggle of financial responsibility for themselves (Tanner & Arnett, 2009, 2011). Emerging adults are willing to undertake the financial responsibility associated with independence in order to engage in their successful transition into adulthood. Carlos highlights the difficulty, but importance, of this realization:

> Honestly, just really, the turning point was me realizing that I had to fend for myself and I had to work for everything that I have and that I have to get. So, that just made me realize, wow, nobody's going to do it, so I have to do it. Nobody's helping me out so I have to figure it out. And I've been figuring it out. Ain't the easiest road, but I'd say that was a turning point where my decision too became a little more clearer, I wasn't 100%, but I was getting there, building the blocks.

He acknowledges here that this type of independence, where he must take responsibility for and control of his own financial security, is not easily or quickly achieved. In fact, several of the study participants held a second job to supplement the income they earned from their jobs at the community-based organization. Establishing financial security is necessary for a successful transition into adulthood, and these participants clearly recognized that they had to work hard to establish the type of responsibility indicative of adulthood in this domain.

One aspect of financial responsibility, housing, has a significant meaning for emerging adults. Residential stability, classically considered as home ownership by the criminological literature, is a proven turning point for young people engaging in reentry or desistance. While this serves as an important marker of the transition to adulthood, securing housing either as a renter or homeowner is also a fundamental need. This differentiates residential stability and its role in desistance from other turning points, such as marriage, parenthood, or potentially even employment. Housing additionally represents an important step of independence within financial responsibility, where emerging adults can establish a space as their own. They want to enjoy the benefits of using the space as they wish (i.e., inviting over friends, not needing permission from others) but also accept the responsibility that comes along with establishing independent housing (i.e., paying for this housing).

Young people leaving the justice system are more likely to experience housing instability, often moving frequently (i.e., after a few weeks or months) or being unable to secure housing (Abrams & Terry, 2017; Fader, 2013; Harding & Harris, 2020). This most certainly influences how they are able to desist and transition into prosocial adulthood. Sean discussed the importance of housing within desistance when talking about support he sees his peers needing:

> ... with people worrying about where they next spot to sleep at or they next meal, your mentality ... you ain't really in the right mindset. You feel what I'm saying? It could just mess up your day, just that, not knowing where your next spot to stay or next meal or something is at.

Sean recognizes that housing, and food security, serves as a fundamental need for young people. For Sean, this was an area he wished both the community-based organization and the justice system would provide young people more assistance with to help support their desistance.

Around half of the participants in this sample experienced residential instability or insecurity within their desistance processes. This included being kicked out, or not welcomed back into, the homes of their families, couch surfing, or losing their apartments. Some of the participants expressed that they were not able to return to previous housing situations because of their engagements in crime, deviance, and/or drug use. They had burned some of these bridges, so to speak, with family, friends, roommates, and romantic partners who were not as willing to provide housing for someone who had betrayed them or their trust (Fader, 2013).

Other participants, like Kareem, acknowledge that they cannot return to live where they grew up as it may threaten their desistance process, their successful reentry, or even their life. When discussing going back to visit his family in a town about a half hour from where he currently lives, Kareem emphasizes:

> Now I got to keep turning back where I'm going to be looking behind my back to see who's there or not. Out here in [this new city] I can be walking up the street… and I don't have to be looking backwards because I know I'm going to be safe. I don't have nobody coming after me.

Even though he feels safer in his current city, he has struggled to make a home for himself there. Kareem recognizes that he does not like being so removed from his family and the community he grew up in, but that it is also a necessity for his life and his desistance.

Most participants specifically identified establishing housing independent of their parents or families as an important turning point into adulthood. This marker is particularly important within financial stability as it signifies autonomy in the relationship between emerging adults and their parents or families (Arnett, 2000, 2016; Tanner & Arnett, 2009). Sebastian, for example, is currently living at his mother's house, and previously had lived with a romantic partner. He hopes to get his own home in a few years:

> I want, at thirty, I want my own little spot. Like, "This is my house. Come to my house." Not, "Is it okay with your girl, or your mom?" "Nah. Come to my house." Feel me?

Sebastian expresses here that he wants a home where he doesn't have to get permission to invite friends over, his "own little spot". Interestingly, Sebastian (currently 24) sets the goal for this turning point at the age of 30, signifying a delay in own perceptions of when this turning point can be achieved from theorizations of establishing residentially stability and/or home ownership. For Sebastian, this future goal of establishing an independent living situation serves as an important marker of his own successful transition into adulthood.

Generally, participants recognized that a longer-term version of financial stability meant for adulthood was distinct from the type of financial stability they were aiming for currently within emerging adulthood. Successful, longer-term monetary stability was defined by markers such as owning a home, owning a car, or establishing monetary savings. Kareem, who earlier identified in his interview as wanting to become a paramedic, further elaborates on this theme:

> It's like paramedic is not going to cut it. I can't have that job and buy a Bugatti or buy a Lamborghini, or I can't buy, you know what I mean, the house that I want. If it's like that, I don't know. I said I want to get into business. While I'm being a paramedic, I can still be going to school, and I can still look into further stuff. Just owning my own properties, I would like to own my own properties out here.

Here, Kareem admits that becoming a paramedic is not his final career goal but understands that this job provides a more immediate stepping stone in establishing responsibility on the way to achieving his longer-term goals.

Kareem believes that becoming a paramedic is a satisfying and meaningful career he can take on while also making a positive impact on the community. He states here that as a paramedic, he can continue to further his education in order to expand his future career options in service of his long-term monetary stability and success characterized by owning a business, property, and cars. Kareem, thus, acknowledges that although this process may not be quick or easy, he is willing to put the long-term work into achieving his goals of financial success. In addition, he believes that this process of achieving financial success and working can still be enjoyable, which is in line with the general literature on emerging adulthood.

As Steve describes here, responsibility can extend beyond the financial and into other cultural norms and markers for adults. While owning a car or even a home is important for him, something as simple as getting his driver's license may even serve to fulfill this domain of responsibility:

> I really just want to make something of myself. I don't know. Just be able to have my own house, own my own car, because even sometimes still, I'm like, "I'm never gonna own my own car." But I don't know. That's something big for me I want to be able to do. I don't have my license. I never went. I'm 25. I just never went and got it, tried to get it. Just jail and stuff like that always holding me back. So just to be able to go and get my license, that would be a big deal, too. You know?

Here, Steve equates the tasks of getting his driver's license and owning a car or home with "making something" of himself, serving as an identity project for him within his maturation. These tasks represent an aspect of success in achieving responsibility within society and are in line with cultural norms. While these participants view owning a car, owning a home, and establishing savings as important markers of responsibility, identity projects and other markers like getting a driver's license, becoming a paramedic, or having their "own spot" may aid self-perceptions of maturity for young people facing barriers in their desistance and successful transitions into adulthood.

Perspective

The third domain of **perspective** represents the consciousness of a young person, including their ability to understand the complexity of social situations and interpret them from multiple viewpoints (Steinberg & Cauffman, 1996; see also Gottfredson & Hirschi, 1990). Within this sample, many of the participants expressed how this consciousness directly influenced their behaviors. Often, in these examples where young people exhibit maturity within the domain of perspective, it overlaps with the domains of temperance and responsibility. For young people, the development of perspective also includes establishing an orientation toward the future, including hopes and goals for their future selves. This is an important feature of psychosocial maturity unique to emerging adulthood and distinguishing it from other phases of the life course (e.g., adolescence; Galambos & Costigan, 2003; Galambos et al., 2005; Droppelmann, 2021).

Progress within the domain of responsibility, and in particular the commitment to autonomy and financial stability, builds into this domain of perspective for emerging adults. For instance, participants expressed that building a family is an important example of their future orientation and their commitment to engaging in prosocial society. Through building a stable household, participants tie their commitment to societal norms with their attachment to the family within the context of their life story. This household serves as an important marker for their future successful transition into adulthood. Diego expresses how this goal is important for him:

> I see me just taking care of my daughter, my family. Just trying to get my own apartment. I don't see nothing else in my life but my daughter honestly.

For him, building a family and providing a home for them is his main goal and an important indicator of his achievement of maturity across both the domains of responsibility and perspective.

Many other participants expressed engaging in similar actions of working to build their own happy families. Mateo, for example, describes this when discussing the next chapter in his life's story:

> Well, my son, he lives in [another state] right now with my baby mom, but I just flew them out here. They're about to come out here next week. I got them their flight stuff. It's looking pretty bright. I'm going to be with my family.

Participants are committed to establishing an idealized nuclear family, where they can build a family with a partner under their own roof. For several participants, leaving a "legacy" for their children, such as a business or a home, was integral to this domain of perspective. When discussing his hopes for the future, Sebastian states that he wants to own a business but is unsure of exactly what type of business. He follows this up by saying, "I know I want something to be left for my kids when I die. A little business for them to keep running for themselves, or something". This sentiment indicates the desire to leave a prosocial legacy for children and links to a theme of **generativity**, as the participants express leaving this legacy for their children as a part of their transition into adulthood (Erikson, 1950, 1963; Maruna, 2001; McAdams & de St. Aubin, 1992; McAdams et. al, 1998). Thus, achieving markers of maturity within the domain of responsibility alone may not be enough to facilitate the transition into adulthood for all emerging adults. Sequencing this maturation into the domain of perspective may be imperative for self-perceptions of maturation.

Participants also provided similar examples of how maturity in this domain of perspective was linked to their maturity within the domain of temperance. Diego provides a particularly poignant example of this from an incident where he was robbed at gunpoint by another young person whom he knew:

Diego: I got robbed at gunpoint, I knew the kid, I knew where he was at, where he stayed at. I went over there, I went to him. Like, he, I felt like he had my life in his hands, so I wanted to have his life in my hands at the moment. I had all these n****s hyping me up and shit. But then like I started thinking about the bigger picture. Like I was right in front of him, kind of, like he didn't see me but I seen him, the guy that robbed me. So just sitting there I can do whatever I want to this guy right now, you know what I mean. I can do whatever I want to him right now. Like, you know what I mean, but I just turned around and walked away.

Interviewer: Why did you turn around and walk away?

Diego: Because like I said I wasn't thinking about myself. So sometimes it's good, like I say sometimes it's good and sometimes it's bad.

Interviewer: So you were thinking about him?

Diego: I was thinking about everybody. I was thinking about him, about his mom, what my mom would think if this would be happening to me. You know what I mean, how my mom would feel, how my family would feel, you know what I mean. I didn't want to go to jail obviously. I just didn't want to put that pressure on everybody. I didn't want to put that pressure on my family I didn't want to put that pressure on his family. It's just like you know there's a whole bunch of shit that can go wrong at the moment.

Here, Diego emphasizes a moment where he exhibits psychosocial maturity across domains of temperance and perspective together. He recognizes the complexity of this situation and is able to examine it from several viewpoints, demonstrating maturity within the domain of perspective. Additionally, he is then able to translate this into his decision-making and behaviors, demonstrating maturity within the domain of temperance. Importantly, Diego also recognizes the importance of this moment within his own identity. As Diego's earlier quote in this chapter expressed "I'm not a little kid, I'm a grown ass man, I do grown ass man shit". For Diego, this "grown ass man shit" is evidenced by his self-control, his ability to avoid peer pressure to engage in deviance, and his active choice to avoid retaliation through violence. These integrate to reinforce maturation across the domains of temperance and perspective together, amplifying the effect of these self-perceptions of maturation and identity.

Conclusion

Across theories of emerging adulthood and criminology, maturation operates as an important mechanism for influencing the successful development of young people across the life course. While operationalized in many ways, maturation theories are grounded in three main components: sociological, psychological, and biological. This chapter focused on psychological, or cognitive, maturation through two domains codified under the work of Rocque (2012, 2015) and colleagues (Rocque et al., 2015, 2016, 2019): Cognitive Transformation/Identity Maturation and Psychosocial Maturation.

The domain of cognitive transformation and identity maturation encompasses self-perceptions and one's attitudes toward social institutions, including the changes one experiences as they mature through the life course. For emerging adults, delineating one's younger self from their current (or hoped-for future) self was central to their cognitive transformation. Participants were able to express changes in both their self-perceptions and attitudes toward deviance as evidence of their own maturation. By recognizing that they were growing up, their identities within their own narratives shifted, allowing them to embrace redemption narratives and the desistance process.

The domain of psychosocial maturation encompasses one's adaptive functioning and socioemotional competence. This domain is conceptualized through three categories: temperance, responsibility, and perspective. First, temperance covers examples of rationality, self-control, and reductions in aggression and impulsivity as indicative of one's maturation across the life course. Second, responsibility covers examples of independence and autonomy as indicative of maturation. For emerging adults, this often centers around independence from family, including financial independence. Third, perspective is grounded in the development of consciousness and an orientation toward the future, including establishing goals for one's future.

Across all three categories, participants provided evidence in their narratives of the development of their own adaptive functioning and socioemotional competence. They presented examples of how they have developed across these domains within their processes of growing up and maturing. These included examples such as exercising self-control in situations where they previously would have been violent, working toward establishing financial independence from parents, and thinking about the consequences of their actions on their future goals. Maturation under the psychosocial domain plays an important role in how these young people recognize their own development and maturation across the life course.

While these examples of cognitive maturation are important for the development of young people and in particular for those working on desisting, these examples largely occur within a social context. Cognitive maturation, for example, in terms of curbing impulsivity, establishing financial security, and changing attitudes toward social institutions, offers just one piece of the maturation process. Emerging adults must take these cognitive maturations and apply them in the contexts and constraints of their social existence. In the subsequent two chapters, I work to examine maturation across sociological domains for these justice-involved emerging adults, including in their relationships and in their engagements with social institutions.

5

RELATIONSHIPS AND SOCIAL SUPPORTS

Every young person has their own individual trajectory through the life course, engaging in the cognitive processes of identity change and maturation. These trajectories, however, are not grounded solely in the individual, as they occur within the social context of that young person's life (Hagestad & Settersten, 2017). Relationships play a vital role in a young person's social role maturation across the life course. A person's connections to others often shape their experiences in the world including what they believe, how they spend their time, and how they behave. This is especially true within the understanding of desistance across the life course, where the connections young people have can motivate them to either engage in deviance or desist from crime. Individual trajectories, thus, are not exclusively individual but contain a social context that when neglected may lead to incomplete conclusions about development across the life course (Hagestad & Settersten, 2017; Settersten, 2018).

Within the desistance literature, the discussion of the influence of social support on desistance has largely been grounded in the life stages of youth and adolescence. Criminologists have begun to extend this perspective to examine how these theoretical influences fare under emerging adulthood theory. As such, they have found mixed support for the application of classical operationalizations of relationships within studying young adult desistance. For example, Salvatore and Taniguchi (2012) present evidence that parental attachment, marriage, and being a parent contribute to desistance among emerging adults. However, Lloyd and Turanovic (2020) find that attachment to parents did not contribute to their cessation of drug and alcohol use.

In this chapter I will extend theorizations of the impact of relationships and social supports on desistance for emerging adults using theory from the

DOI: 10.4324/9781003143581-6

field and evidence from my interviews for this research. Importantly, my goal in this work is to codify turning points grounded in social support under the interdisciplinary lens of both emerging adulthood theory and life course criminology. Thus, as I present evidence from my own research, I work to compare this to evidence from existing theory and research. Generally, several themes across the domain of Adult Social Role maturation emerged within the evidence from the stories shared by participants in my sample. Many of these themes were able to be categorized into traditional groupings (i.e., Parents/family, Friends/peers, Romantic Relationships, Children).

Relationships in Emerging Adulthood

Social experiences offer opportunities within which to develop or dismantle relationships in accordance with one's progression through the life course (Kreager et al., 2018; Marsden, 2018). Within the life stage of emerging adulthood, changes in social networks are both expected and encouraged. This includes an exploration of who is in one's social circle, allowing young people to embrace the opportunity to make new social ties or redefine preexisting relationships. Largely, this is attributed to changes within the context of the transition from adolescence to emerging adulthood, where emerging adults now have different mechanisms and expectations for their social relationships, familial relationships, and connections to social institutions.

The literature on emerging adulthood has found evidence that the context and content of relationships are distinct from adolescence (Arnett, 2000, 2016). As young adults explore their place in the world and their own belief systems, they are also transitioning out of the stability of adolescence. For example, as young people become adults, they are no longer required to live with their parents or to attend school. This forces young people into a period of instability in their connection with social institutions. Often, emerging adults are looking to establish independence from their parents in their path to adulthood. Additionally, they continue to explore friendships and romantic relationships in an effort to determine what they want for the permanency of adulthood (e.g., Allan, 2008; Barry et al., 2016; Shulman & Connolly, 2016). For some young people, it is easy to make these changes in certain domains and difficult to make these changes in others.

Much of this instability is unique for emerging adults compared to young people of similar ages in previous generations. Millennials and members of Generation Z are more likely to participate in higher education (i.e., community college, college, university), delaying starting a career in favor of continued learning and exploration (Magolda & Taylor, 2016; Marshall & Butler, 2016). Additionally, young people in these generations have a higher average age of marriage, becoming a parent, and becoming a homeowner (Vespa, 2017). This is explained under emerging adulthood theory by shifts in cultural norms. For example, as young people age out of adolescence, traditionally they commit to romantic partners (often via marriage) in their late teens or early 20s on average (King et al., 2007). Emerging adults, however, continue to engage in exploration of romantic partners well into their 20s on average (Shulman & Connolly, 2016). These changes in social expectations affect how young people can embrace turning points into adulthood.

Additionally, new domains of online communities and social networking websites influence how emerging adults interact with others and form or maintain their relationships. Technology and social media may offer a means by which young people can craft or reinforce their social identity during this transitional phase (e.g., Subrahmanyam et al., 2008; Yang et al., 2017). Emerging adults likely have close friendships or communities they interact with either partially or completely through technology such as social media, texting, or email (e.g., Bobkowski & Smith, 2013; Fox & Warber, 2013; Subrahmanyam et al., 2008). This affects how social and structural components of community impact the transition into adulthood for young people. In turn, this may influence how young adults connect to their social networks and present their identity to others, shaping how they think others perceive them and their role in society.

Parents and Families

Families represent one of the most significant relationship types within a young person's life. As young people age out of adolescence, they experience changes in their expectations of and needs of their parents and families. For emerging adults, the crux of this change lies within establishing autonomy from parents. Emerging adulthood theory postulates that establishing independence and autonomy, such as financial independence from parents, is important for young people to view themselves as adults (Arnett, 2000, 2016). This is distinct from adolescence, where a strong and dependent relationship with parents is theorized as important for facilitating social control. Instead, within emerging adulthood, the relationship between parents and their emerging adult children improves when the emerging adult can establish this autonomy (Dubas & Petersen, 1996; Fingerman et al., 2011; Fingerman & Yahirun, 2016; O'Connor et al., 1996), changing its function as a social control.

This change is largely attributed to the shift in the role parents play in the life of the emerging adult (Aquilino, 2006; Johnson et al., 2011). As an adolescent, parents can form robust relationships with their kids by providing them with support – both emotional and material (e.g., housing, financial). Upon entering emerging adulthood, the expectations and needs of families and parents change. Emerging adults shift the focus of these relationships away from material support and toward an emphasis on emotional support. Emerging adults want to establish autonomy from their parents to make their own choices and establish material independence (e.g., housing, financial). As autonomy from parents increases for emerging adults, it may improve the positive attachment young people feel toward their parents (Dubas & Petersen, 1996; O'Connor et al., 1996). Importantly, emerging adulthood theory still emphasizes the importance of emotional support that parents provide (Arnett, 2000, 2016). Emotional support and attachment remain the critical factors of the shift in relationships during this life phase (Copp et al., 2019; Giordano et al., 2007; Johnson et al., 2011).

This shift has important implications for the consideration of social controls and the role of familial relationships within the context of desistance. For adolescents, the material support provided by parents, in addition to the emotional or personal connection with them, serves to support desistance. Adolescents rely on their parents in both ways and risk losing this emotional and material support by engaging in deviance or refusing desistance. As emerging adults focus on autonomy from their parents and work to become less materially reliant on them, this shifts the theoretical mechanisms of familial relationships as a social control (Copp et al., 2019).

Sebastian describes here the influence of his relationship with his mother, who has provided him with support and housing throughout his history of justice-involvement and incarceration, on his behavior:

> The most important relationship right now is my mother, me and my mother. I don't know. I feel like whatever I can do to make her day easier, or better, or whatever, I'm going to do it. Just for her. I wouldn't do that for any other person in my life.

The sentiment of adjusting behavior for the sake of pleasing family (or trying not to displease them), especially parents, rings true for many participants in the sample. Importantly, here Sebastian also emphasizes the reciprocity in the relationship and his role in it. He recognizes the support he has received from his mother and wants to do what he can to ensure that he recognizes the value of this support.

Dylan provides another example of this theme of adjusting behavior to please family. He explains that in the past he enjoyed spending money on things like cars and vacations and often turned to criminal activity in order to fund his spending habits. These spending habits, however, made his parents upset. He explains that his parents have provided him support throughout his involvement with the justice system and expresses that he doesn't want to make his parents upset and threaten this relationship with continued criminal behavior:

> I want them to be happy. I don't want them to be upset with my decisions. I don't want them to think that I'm gonna waste all my money on stupid things.

Dylan and Sebastian are both aware of how their behaviors, when viewed as controversial or displeasing by parents, affect how they maintain these relationships. They identify that by changing their behaviors to be more in line with their parents' expectations or wishes, they can help to foster a better relationship with their parents (Girodano et al., 2007). This improved relationship is integral to each of their desistance and maturation narratives.

One of the largest barriers these emerging adults face in their maturation is establishing material autonomy from their parents. When compared with their peers, justice-involved emerging adults struggle to separate financially from family, in particular when establishing residential independence (Harding & Harris, 2020; Warner & Remster, 2021). Several of the participants here, such as Sebastian and Dylan, moved back in with their parents after their release from incarceration. Both young men were working to establish enough financial independence to move out, and indicated this was an important step in their path of growing up. But, due to the barriers of incarceration, this progress is often impeded. This may in turn threaten the success of the cognitive maturation young people engage in within their transition to adulthood and desistance in their social contexts. As Sebastian and Dylan both indicate above though, they are working to compensate for this by demonstrating maturity in their behaviors and interactions with their parents.

Being the eldest in his family, Mateo acknowledges that serving as a role model to his siblings influences how he presents himself and behaves around them, in order to guide how they develop:

Mateo: My siblings, they look at me like their father because they know their dad wasn't around for them. They're very young too, so they don't even know what their father looks like. They see me, and they see their older brother, like this is the n****r we know as our father. They love me. Every time they see me, they hugging me. Like I said, they see their dad. They're special to me. But I just don't have a good relationship with my mom. I don't really see my brothers and sisters like that.

Interviewer: Do you sometimes change the way that you act because you know they're looking up to you?

Mateo: I don't act crazy around them, or stupid, because I know they'll copy me. Definitely. They like to copy. They already do that. They copy what people do. I just imagine if I was swearing around them, and then they'll repeat it.

He acknowledges how he serves as a role model for his younger siblings and an understanding that they are aware of and may even imitate his behaviors. Here, the role of an older brother facilitates some self-regulation of his behavior. Additionally, this behavior modeling, or generativity, serves to advance his transition into adulthood (Erikson, 1950; 1963; Maruna, 2001; McAdams & de St. Aubin, 1992; McAdams et. al, 1998) as he acts as a role model and caregiver for his younger siblings. For emerging adults in this role, this type of self-regulation is important around family members in order to avoid further jeopardizing these relationships.

Regarding his family, Daniel acknowledges their support in his desistance process, stating "They just give me this type of motivation. They want to see me successful". He later elaborates on the depth of his attachments in relation to his past:

> They seen when I was at my lowest, I was in the streets, I was doing bad things. I was getting into a lot of trouble. They rather see me doing something for myself. They don't want to see me doing the same things and falling into the same predicaments.

Here, Daniel acknowledges that his family has seen him experience low points in his life, including his entanglement in the justice system. Yet, they are still supportive and hopeful for his future. He is aware that they would rather see him embrace prosocial roles instead of returning to engagement in risky behaviors.

Diego echoes a similar sentiment here regarding his family, stating:

> Because at the end of the day those are the people that are always going to be there for me, no matter what. Those are the people that are going to be there for me no matter what. If I need a couple dollars, I can call my dad, and he'll send me some money. If I need to go get away from something I can go to my little brother's room and chill with him for a little while, you know what I mean... My mom is never going to let me starve, my mom helps me every day with my daughter. If the nights are too long, in the morning time my mom will wake up and she'll come take my daughter, let her sleep. It's just like the little stuff that matters, the little stuff that a lot of people don't get from their parents, their family.

Here, Diego identifies several types of support he receives from different family members: money from his father, friendship from his brother, food and help caring for his daughter from his mother. For him, this "little stuff" that he gets from his family is what is most important about these attachments. While some of this support, like being fed by his mother, may seem material, it is grounded in more of an emotional context as his mom "is never going to let [him] starve". While financial autonomy is important for emerging adults, the lines are blurred when establishing this autonomy threatens access to basic resources like food and shelter. This type of family support remains pivotal for the desistance narratives of participants who value family among their strongest attachments. Family provides these participants with the support, accountability, and opportunity to transition out of their criminal past and into a prosocial adulthood.

Friends and Peers

The social support of and connection to peers has long been identified as important for youth. For emerging adults, this importance persists, but the context of these relationships shifts. As this period in the life course is defined by much change, friendships and the support they provide are important in adapting to these changes (Barry et al., 2016). Friends often fill the gap created during exploration between the childhood family and establishing an adult family (via partnership and parenthood), making peer groups a primary support for emerging adults (Allan, 2008; Demir & Özdemir, 2010; Guan & Fuligni, 2016).

The importance of friendship and the potential adjustment of peer groups during the exploration of emerging adulthood are important indicators of the developmental process (Barry et al., 2016), reflecting the changes in social roles for this stage in the life course (Carstensen et al., 1999). Unlike adolescents who often seek a large number of friends or acquaintances for their social network, emerging adults shift their focus to a smaller group of closer friends. Friendship in emerging adulthood becomes largely grounded in the concept of emotional support. Emerging adults are working to identify and secure friendships with people they can rely on and trust (Allan, 2008; Demir & Özdemir, 2010; Guan & Fuligni, 2016). This is especially important for young adults engaging in desistance, who depend on this support of friends to facilitate identity change and desistance (Mawson et al., 2015).

The literature on desistance has consistently found that **cutting ties**, or "'knifing off' the unwanted past" (Elder, 1998, p. 966), with criminogenic social networks (i.e., peers, family, acquaintances) is central to embracing turning points (e.g., Caspi & Moffitt, 1993; Farrall, 2002; Laub & Sampson, 2003; Maruna & Roy, 2007; Warr, 2002). Through this process of cutting criminogenic ties, youth engaged in deviance can craft their social networks to facilitate their desistance process. Cutting criminogenic ties facilitates the transition into new life roles through turning points, often allowing youth to separate their desisting selves from their previously criminal selves (Laub & Sampson, 2003). This provides an opportunity for young people to mature into a more satisfactory, prosocial adulthood (Rocque, 2015).

Participants in this study expressed that cutting ties with old friends who did not support their desistance was necessary for their transition into prosocial adult roles. Themes of trust, loyalty, and support emerged as qualities they expect out of their social networks. Relationships that do not contain these qualities were deemed detrimental to their desistance and participants expressed a desire to cut or "knife" them out of their social networks. The knifing off process, however, may not be the same for all social ties, as participants noted that they still placed values on certain ties with people who are involved in deviance. Therefore, trimming these networks may not be as simple for emerging adults when compared to adolescents whose relationships may be less permanent.

Sebastian expresses this clearly in his effort to refine his social network through cutting ties with "fake ass friends" who used to "push [him] to do some dumb shit over and over". He acknowledges that these friends are not trustworthy and do not have his best interest at heart. He provides an example here of how he would rather be alone and know that he is secure than be surrounded by people he cannot trust:

> I'd rather be by myself chilling in my crib, on my porch, whatever, listening to some music. By myself. Knowing that I'm good. If I shit my pants right now, chilling on my porch, I shit my pants, I'm with nobody. This n****r can't tell nobody. But if I'm with somebody, I'm like, "This n****r probably going to tell a bitch that I shit my pants." Knowing that I'm safe, whatever I do right now, it come falling down with doing a crime. Are you with somebody that's fake? When they get caught, they going to tell on you? It all comes down, even with little things in life that I experience with fake people.

Sebastian provides this example of a potentially embarrassing moment that he wouldn't want shared with others as a metaphor for trust. If something embarrassing were to happen to him, he would rather experience it alone than do so with people whom he cannot trust and who might reveal this information to others. This reflects the importance of trust and loyalty in friendship for emerging adults, who now rely on friends as a primary support group (Allan, 2008). This understanding of friendship offers an important indicator of the developmental process for emerging adults (Barry et al., 2016) and the new social roles emerging adults engage in (Carstensen et al., 1999).

Sebastian continues to acknowledge that not everyone will be "fake" or untrustworthy:

> Not everybody's going to be like that. Not everybody. 75, 90%, yeah. But it's like a little 10%, 15% of real people are like you. Like you, that will love you the same way you love them. Cherish the friendship like you do. If I call you my brother, if you're my friend, I don't call you a friend no more. You're my brother, my family. You're family.

What he highlights is that the most important social connections he has should be treated as such. Sean shares the same perspective as Sebastian, stating "Some of my relatives ain't my family". He also recognizes the ability to select who is considered family, whether with actual relatives or friends and peers, is based on the quality of the relationship. This group in the inner social circle, or the chosen "family", is recognized for their importance. Through cutting criminogenic or antisocial ties, participants acknowledge that they are instead able to focus on these more important prosocial connections and prefer to transfer their efforts into maintaining these relationships.

Cutting ties with close connections, however, may not always be easy. Relationships with friends who are engaged in crime or other risky behaviors are often still valued because of the deep connections they have formed (Copp et al., 2019). When these relationships are valued and emerging adults may not want to cut the ties completely, they may still attempt to remove them from within their inner social circle. When talking about his friends and their influence on his behaviors, Daniel expresses:

> Some of them, like I said, they just so into that lifestyle, they don't want to change. But you know, those are my friends. I still ... that's their decision, I respect it, but, as long as you don't bring me down with you, then it can keep it on a friendship, you know. I don't want ... I got friends that are in and out of jail. I know they're my friend, and they know I'm their friend, but we live two different lives. So, they always in and out of jail. I don't want to be that friend that goes down with them, and then now I'm in and out of jail. I rather just keep my distance basically and do better for myself.

Here, Daniel highlights the value of these relationships, while acknowledging that these friends are engaged in criminal activity. Through understanding that he and his friends are living "two different lives", he is able to reconcile the value he places on these relationships while pulling away from these friendships. Overall, separating from or cutting these ties with social connections who may threaten desistance is central to these participants' desistance narratives.

For emerging adults, this process of cutting criminogenic ties is central to the transition into adulthood and embracement of turning points out of crime (e.g., Laub & Sampson, 2003). Cutting these ties allows emerging adults to avoid peers who may encourage deviance and instead embrace new roles and turning points in their life course. In lieu of maintaining these ties, emerging adults now focus on maintaining bonds with people who are loyal, trustworthy, and supportive (Allan, 2008; Barry et al., 2016; Salvatore, 2017). This new focus is one that demarcates social connections among friends and peers, likely extending into the realm of romantic relationships for emerging adults as well.

Romantic Relationships

Romantic relationships are posited as one of the most important during youth, and in particular for supporting desistance. While young people begin dating within adolescence, they still view this period of dating as primarily recreational (Arnett, 2000; Roscoe et al., 1987) and temporary, allowing for the exploration of romantic love and sexual experiences (Arnett, 2000; Feiring, 1996). Romantic experiences in adolescence are often shorter and may exist within the context of social activities (Arnett, 2000). Criminologists have often linked this dating and romantic exploration within adolescence with an increased opportunity for unstructured socializing, risky behaviors, and involvement with delinquent peers (see Seffrin et al., 2009, for a review). Through dating and involvement with multiple romantic partners, youth may also internalize an identity as a "troublemaker" (Seffrin et al., 2009).

Within the life course perspective, marriage has been one of the most pervasive findings among relationships that support the desistance process. Criminologists have consistently found ample evidence that marriage supports the desistance process (e.g., Bersani et al., 2009; Craig & Foster, 2013; Horney et al., 1995; Laub et al., 1998; Sampson & Laub, 1993; Sampson et al., 2006). Romantic relationships and marriage often play a role in facilitating the development of turning points beyond this attachment, such as seeking stable employment or cutting criminogenic ties (King et al., 2007; Warr, 1998). This evidence has even translated into the study of young and emerging adults in the desistance process, with marriage maintaining its role as one of the strongest prosocial attachments (Chassin et al., 2002; Labouvie, 1996; Marcus, 2009; Piquero et al., 2002).

However, as socio-structural changes in society have facilitated an increased average age of marriage for young people, this threatens if and how dating and marriage can continue to play a role as a turning point for desistance. Dating extends later into the life course for the typical Millennial and now with Generation Z, providing an opportunity to explore the potential trajectory and goals of romantic relationships (Arnett, 2000). Within the transition into emerging adulthood, romantic explorations become more intimate, with the focus of these relationships shifting toward physical and emotional intimacy. Compared to adolescence, these relationships tend to last longer and may involve cohabitation, with an emphasis toward intimacy and exploring the qualities and characteristics desired of a life partner (Arnett, 2000; Forrest, 2014; Shulman & Connolly, 2016). However, when a young person experiences an end to one of these romantic relationships, it provides an opportunity for increased risky behaviors or substance use (Jang & Rhodes, 2012).

Therefore, during this life phase, dating and romantic exploration take on a very different role for young people than within adolescence. Romantic exploration becomes normalized during emerging adulthood (Arnett, 2000; Feiring, 1996; Roscoe et al., 1987; Shulman & Connolly, 2016), affording young people the opportunity to engage with different partners while limiting self-perceptions of immaturity. Although the strength of this effect may not reach that of marriage, dating within emerging adulthood and its characteristics (e.g., cohabitation) can still facilitate greater stability and support prosocial behaviors (Arnett, 2000; Forrest, 2014; Shulman & Connolly, 2016).

The majority of participants in this sample discussed romantic relationships and their experiences with romance throughout their life story interviews. Generally, participants discussed their experimentation with romantic relationships and their learning experiences after breakups. However, rarely did these participants identify romantic relationships as among their most important attachments. Only two of the participants – Diego and Steve – expressed their goals of trying to establish a stable life with their current partners.

Diego discussed the process of falling in love with his current girlfriend, which he was extremely resistant to when they first met. He has just come out of a tumultuous breakup with another woman and expressed that he was not interested in settling down with a partner. He discussed how in this new romantic connection with his current girlfriend, he "[did not] want to be in a relationship no more". When his new girlfriend would express to Diego that she loved him, Diego said he would tell her back that he was not in love and did not want to continue into a serious relationship.

However, Diego notes that this was occurring during a major low point for him, where he had quit his involvement with the community-based organization, was using drugs, and not working. He began to recognize that his girlfriend was offering a positive and prosocial support system that he needed:

> She just stood by me. I couldn't give her no food, I couldn't give her no nothing... that's what we ate every day, just one meal, when my mom cooks. That's it. She's not complaining. She's not telling me nothing. She's not arguing with me, you know. ... I can't brush that off, because I'm doing really bad and she's just here by my side this whole time.... As much as I want to, I can't brush that off.

For Diego, this turning point was realizing that she "actually liked me as a person, she didn't like what I had, because I didn't have nothing". Diego expresses how this was a major turning point for him:

> From there I took off. You know I just ran with it. Then I started working at [a restaurant], I think. I started making really good money... But I didn't have a car, so I had to come back to [the community-based organization] ... you know how [they] help you in all types of ways.

After returning to the community-based organization, Diego's girlfriend became pregnant, which only increased his motivation to support her both financially and emotionally.

This theme of support and love in the face of drug use and justice-system involvement echoes in Steve's narrative as well. When he first met his current girlfriend, he was worried that she would judge him for his past drug use. But after sharing his experience with her, Steve said "it made me full, feel more comfortable". He discussed how as their relationship developed and she became pregnant, it became further motivation for him to "get clean" and avoid "catch[ing] a new case" in the system. It even motivated him to turn himself into the court for a warrant, so that he could serve his sentence because he was worried that he "might not have been home when my son was being born".

Outside of the narratives of Diego and Steve, none of the other participants discussed romantic partners as important to their desistance processes. Importantly, even for Diego and Steve, having a child with their partner served as an important facilitator for the role of the romantic relationship in the desistance process. This may suggest that romantic relationships alone in this life stage may not be enough to act as a facilitator for desistance among justice-involved emerging adults. This is consistent with the general literature on emerging adulthood, which proposes that this developmental period is characterized by temporary and exploratory romantic relationships (Arnett, 2000; Feiring, 1996; Roscoe et al., 1987; Shulman & Connolly, 2016). However, this diverges from traditional perspectives within criminology, which place a heavy emphasis on romantic relationships and marriage supporting desistance (e.g., Laub et al., 1998; Sampson & Laub, 1993).

The delay of marriage until the late 20s for adults (Arnett, 2000, 2016; Furstenberg et al., 2005; Shanahan, 2000) may be a large factor contributing to this change in the importance of marriage for justice-involved emerging adults. In addition, there may be a change in the hierarchy of turning points for emerging adults. Stability within other turning points, such as employment or housing, may be necessary prior to justice-involved emerging adults recognizing the role of romantic relationships and marriage for desistance (Nader & Davies Robinson, 2023; Piquero et al., 2002; Salvatore & Taniguchi, 2012). When justice-involved emerging adults face delays in stabilizing within other turning points, this may only serve to continue delaying access to romance as a turning point for this population.

Several participants in this study discussed the need for establishing their own maturity prior to being able to (or being interested in) build a long-term romantic partnership. This maturity centered around topics of both material stability (e.g., a job, independent home) and emotional growth (e.g., "growing up"). Kareem and Dylan, for example, both emphasized their desire to explore romantic relationships in order to understand what they want from a partner, and to figure out how they can be a good partner.

Sebastian, at 24 and among the oldest of the participants, discusses how he learned from a previous breakup with a partner he shared two daughters with. Sebastian and his ex-girlfriend used to live together with their two children. After this breakup, his ex-girlfriend got married to one of his friends. Her new husband then took on a larger role in parenting the children. In the transition from seeing his children every day and being a father to being limited in his contact with his children, this caused tension for Sebastian, eventually leading him back into drug use and justice system involvement.

Now, Sebastian reflects back on this breakup, saying "that's when I knew what I wanted as a person, as a significant other, or even as a friend". Since this tension, Sebastian has become estranged from his two children and his ex-girlfriend, and reflects on missing being a father to his daughters. He now feels that he has a clearer perspective on what he expects out of a future relationship: "if I get with another girl, this is how I want her to act. Then I can further our relationship if she's acting the right way". Several of the other participants, including Emma, echoed the importance of break-ups and how they can make you "stronger" by learning from them.

Together, these examples provide evidence that approaches to romance within emerging adulthood extend the recreational or temporary nature of dating in adolescence (Arnett, 2000; Feiring, 1996; Roscoe et al., 1987). Emerging adults, including those with justice system involvement, engage with romantic exploration as a learning process. These romantic explorations, and the lessons learned from them, become more intimate than in adolescence. The focus shifts toward identifying both what qualities and characteristics they want in a life partner and what kind of life partner they themselves want to be.

Becoming a Parent

The final relationship type explored in this chapter is becoming a parent. Parenthood is another key attachment that facilitates desistance (Laub & Sampson, 2003), the effects of which extend into emerging adulthood (Salvatore & Taniguchi, 2012). Justice-involved young people who do become parents within emerging adulthood are typically working to embrace maturation and adult roles (Abeling-Judge, 2021; Stone & Rydberg, 2019). However, young people overall are delaying the age at which they become parents for the first time (Arnett, 2000, 2016; Shanahan, 2000; Vespa, 2017).

Interestingly, just over half of the participants in this study were parents. Considering that justice-involved young people are often delayed in reaching turning points when compared to their peers, it may be surprising that so many of these emerging adults were parents. However, this may be due to the recruitment and sampling procedure used for these qualitative participants. The young people recruited for this study were all engaged with a community-based organization that emphasized supporting justice-involved young people with children. Nevertheless, this offers important evidence into the context and content of how becoming a parent as an emerging adult contributes to maturation within the transition to adulthood and desistance.

Embracing the role of the caregiver serves as an important marker of the transition into adulthood. In line with literature on identity transformation within the context of desistance, the caregiver role provides scripts for these participants to embrace this identity transformation (Boonstoppel, 2019; Giordano et al., 2002; Rumgay, 2004). Additionally, the caregiver role is reflective of the norms associated with the transition into adulthood and embracement of generativity (see Erikson, 1950, 1963; see also Maruna, 2001; McAdams & de St. Aubin, 1992; McAdams et al., 1998). Generativity allows those embracing or entering adulthood to engage in contributing to the larger sphere of society by modeling behavior for future generations (i.e., children). Therefore, becoming a parent can support desistance as a turning point out of crime and into prosocial adulthood (Sampson & Laub, 1993; Savolainen, 2009; Zoutewelle-Terovan et al., 2014).

Participants viewed the role of being a good parent as indicative of their transition into a conventional adult role. In telling their life stories, participants expressed their desire to be good parents who can be engaged in their children's lives and provide support to their children. Mateo identifies becoming a father as an important turning point into adulthood because he enjoys the feeling of doing things for his child:

Mateo: Through her whole pregnancy, my mind changed, like I'm having a son. I knew it was my kid, so I'm like, gotta change. I gotta change, so I got two jobs I been working and maintaining. I do it for my son. That definitely changed me.

Interviewer: How does that make you feel that you're putting that effort in for your son?

Mateo: I feel great. Just like doing something for my kid just made me feel good. Just made me feel happy. Just knowing that he's fine, that every day that he's good.

For him, becoming a father was providing the motivation to make a change and become more responsible, which included both his involvement with the community-based organization and finding stable employment in the longer term. Through his efforts to embrace desistance, he is working to support his child, which makes him feel happy and helps him to recognize his own process of growing up.

Additionally, when discussing his choices to stop engaging in behaviors that may get him re-incarcerated, he elaborated "Well, I was just thinking about my pregnant baby mom. I go, you can't afford it, especially because she'll be like, you're a deadbeat father. I don't want to deal with that". Mateo acknowledges that his behaviors are being influenced by his status as a father and justify his choices within his desistance narrative. The role of parenting, thus, affords participants like Mateo the opportunity to embrace the "scripts" (Giordano et al., 2002) associated with what a parent is supposed to be doing, providing a framework through which these emerging adults can embrace desistance (Boonstoppel, 2019).

Steve echoes this as well, identifying how having to consider his child in addition to himself was an impetus for change. Here, he describes the high point in his story as becoming a father for the first time:

> It's my first kid too, so it's big. It's just life changing. Now I have to not worry about only me, but him. I have to support him and just before I didn't have to do a lot. I didn't have to go work to have money to buy food for him, diapers. Just being a father. Just being there for him even if it isn't diapers and stuff like that. Just being with him instead of in jail or on the streets.

Here, Steve recognizes that fatherhood is defined by more than monetary support. For him, fatherhood is tied to desistance. If he engages in crime or becomes incarcerated, he would not be able to be the father he wants to be for his child. Thus, taking on the role of fatherhood allows him to embrace desistance within his transition to adulthood (Jian et al., 2022).

Similarly, Zoe, who had been engaged in the justice system as an adolescent, identifies her transition into motherhood as an important role change that facilitated her desistance. When she became pregnant at 16, Zoe was actively participating in criminogenic activities and had recently spent a short time incarcerated in a juvenile facility:

Zoe: So when I found out I was pregnant with my son I didn't know what I wanted to do, but I feel like the smartest choice I did for me was deciding to keep him even though I was so young. It has grown so much character for me, and he's the greatest accomplishment I have. So for me, that's the smartest choice I ever made, because my life could have been completely opposite if I made the dumb choice, which I feel would have been that other choice.

Interviewer: And what do you think ... Where would you be that's different if you had made a different choice?

Zoe: I feel like I would have had more room to make bad decisions. I probably would have ... I feel like the only reason why I grew up out of all that negative stuff I said that I had led me up to [this community-based organization] in the beginning, like getting expelled and all that, I feel like it would have went further on. Because I even ended up in juvie for like 10 days at one point, and I feel like I probably would have been in [prison] right now for all I know, because I would have had so much freedom. I would have never had any responsibilities, and yeah...

Becoming a parent reinforced the concept of responsibility for Zoe because the responsibility shifted from herself to another person. Embracing her role as a parent serves as a marker of her transition into the adult role of caregiver.

For participants, the role of caregiver functions as a catalyst toward the identity transition into adulthood. Participants view providing care to another human as an important marker of their own adulthood. Carlos, for example, acknowledges that his own childhood was not an easy experience because of his relationships with his family. Here, Carlos expresses that he is motivated to change his behaviors, and thus identity, to ensure that his own child has a better upbringing:

> I think of my son's birth as my high point in my life. Just because that made me change the way I was before, and I wasn't really in the right state of mind and that snapped me back to reality. It made me realize I was all alone, and I didn't want him to be alone, and I didn't want him to struggle the way I struggled and whatnot. I wanted him to have the support I didn't. And that's a big part of me because that's ... I haven't had the stability of becoming a greater person than what I am. I'm not saying it's an excuse, it's my choice, it was my decision, but the birth of my son made me change a lot of my life, and made me realize where I could change and better myself. So, that's a high point in my life because it's just, I'm bringing a whole new life into this world. So, gotta smarten up.

As Carlos expresses, this new caregiver role "snapped [him] back into reality". He embraces the opportunity to become a parent and acknowledges that this transition into parenthood has enabled him to make a change in his life. To engage in the transition into his role as a parent, Carlos explains that he is working toward becoming a "better" version of himself – one that does not engage in criminal or other risky behaviors.

When asked to identify his most important relationships, Carlos responded "Honestly only my son. Just because like I said I feel like I'm alone.

That nobody understands me, and he's looking up to me". For Carlos, fatherhood provides an attachment that he feels is distinct from any other relationship he has experienced. He elaborates that he must be the best version of himself and prioritize this relationship with his son over any others:

> So, I gotta be to the best of my ability and he's my number one concern. My number one concern with relations. Honestly, whoever wants to have a relationship with me, as in friends or anything, you have your hand out, I'll put my hand out. Or I'll put my hand out you put your hand out, whatever. But I really don't ... It's just extra having ... Worrying about all that. I love my people, like I said I love my community but it's just you gotta focus on the right thing. Is that person really worth your time and are you as important to them as they are to you?

For these parents, relationships with their children served as a very positive attachment they had formed. It also provides an opportunity for these parents to assess the value of their existing relationships and the reciprocity of support within these relationships. Parenthood, therefore, provides a catalyst for these participants to reassess their attachments, cut potentially criminogenic ties, and embrace turning points that will facilitate their transition into a prosocial adulthood.

Parenthood is also characterized as being grounded in feelings of love and happiness, as Diego expresses here:

> When my girlfriend, when she got pregnant, I didn't know if I really wanted to have a baby with her. I didn't tell nobody that. Everybody was so happy, I didn't know if I was ready to have a baby though. I didn't know if I was ready for it financially, anything like in all areas, I didn't know if I was ready for it. Like, I just like I just stopped I wasn't being selfish about it. I was thinking about my mom, she was so happy, I was thinking about my girlfriend's family, they were so happy. So I didn't want to be the one to be like I don't want to have this baby. I feel like that was the best decision I ever made. Just simply because I love my daughter to death, you know what I mean. I will never regret getting my girlfriend pregnant, no matter how ... even if 10 years from now we're not together, she's the worst girl in the world, she turns out the worst baby mom in the world, I will never regret getting her pregnant, you know. She's the best gift I ever got.

Here, Diego acknowledges how he was unsure at first if he was prepared for parenthood. However, he justified overcoming his apprehensions by considering them selfish and instead chose to focus on the happiness this pregnancy has brought his family. Additionally, he characterizes his daughter as being the "best gift" and acknowledges the value of this decision to become a parent. Parenthood ultimately serves as an important catalyst into adulthood for these participants, whose attachment to their children is among the strongest and most important they identify.

Conclusion

Relationships and social support are critical for the social maturation of young people. The networks young people have within their families, peers, and communities shape their experiences in the world, including what they believe, how they view themselves, and the decisions they make. These social supports play a particularly critical role for justice-involved young people as the relationships they have can influence the successes or struggles of their desistance processes. The expectations of these relationships, however, have shifted from previous generations of young people, creating unique conditions for the roles of these relationships as young people leave adolescence and emerge into adulthood.

For emerging adults, shifts in the expectations of parents and families are some of the most drastic from adolescence. Emerging adulthood theory proposes that young people seek to establish autonomy and independence from their parents. This autonomy and independence are important to the identity of these young people as adults. This includes establishing financial independence/stability and independent housing from parents. As they do this, young people work to increase the socioemotional support they receive from the family unit. Participants echoed these propositions of theory in their efforts to establish material independence from parents, while simultaneously working to improve the emotional connections they had with their parents. Together, these elements serve as evidence of cognitive maturation while motivating desistance.

Additionally, friends and peers remain an important social support for young people within the context of desistance as they age out of adolescence and into emerging adulthood. In general, emerging adults work to refine their peer networks, shifting the focus from volume in adolescence to quality in adulthood. Participants echoed this in describing how they value friends whom they can trust. They articulated that they want a small circle of friends who support their own maturation and desistance processes. While identifying trustworthy friends was important, this process also included cutting ties with criminogenic peers when possible as these may threaten progress toward maturation and desistance.

Historically, romantic relationships, and in particular marriage, are some of the most important for facilitating desistance in the life course literature. However, emerging adulthood theory proposes that the importance of these relationships to becoming an adult, and subsequently their function as a turning point, has shifted. Emerging adults perceive romantic relationships as temporary later into the life course than in previous generations of young people. This was evidenced in the narratives of participants, who often excluded listing romantic relationships among their most important relationships. Without the role of romantic partners to support the desistance process, this threatens how criminologists can explain desistance across the life course for cohorts of young people.

Finally, becoming a parent was an important turning point for desistance among participants. This does not come as a surprise given the evidence of this across the criminological literature. However, like romantic relationships, emerging adulthood theory does not emphasize parenthood as an important marker of identity maturation for the average emerging adult. Importantly, in this sample, a majority of participants were parents, and none of these parents were married to the partner with whom they had children. Yet, these children served as important motivations for desistance. Thus, criminologists should continue to consider how becoming a parent can affect the desistance process and work to support young parents trying to desist.

These social relationships overall offer a partial view of the adult social role domain proposed by Rocque and colleagues (2015). The next chapter will expand the examination of sociological maturation to the role of social institutions in the desistance processes of justice-involved emerging adults. In this next chapter, I discuss the remaining components of the adult social role domain – employment and careers – as well as civic and communal maturation.

6

SOCIAL INSTITUTIONS

As emerging adults grow out of adolescence, their engagement with society shifts purposefully. These young people are working to establish their social identities as adults, and often beginning to consider if and how they can contribute to society. This work of role exploration is, again, indicative of emerging adulthood (Arnett, 2000). Emerging adults attempting to discover how they can contribute to society and their communities will naturally engage in role exploration by trying out various types of employment, volunteering, and civic engagement. This type of role exploration is distinct from that of adolescence because emerging adults are undertaking this exploration outside of a structured environment (e.g., K–12 schooling, living with parents).

Young people emerging into adulthood often test out various roles within society during this stage of the life course. How young people select their social involvements, and what they want to get out of these social involvements, has shifted in line with emerging adulthood theory. Millennials, and now Generation Z, are looking to make contributions to society that are meaningful, fulfilling, and satisfying in ways that are unique to their generations and intimately tied into their identity as adults (Arnett, 2004). This exploration affords emerging adults the opportunity to develop knowledge and skills that facilitate a transition into adulthood without forcing them to select a finalized role (Dietrich & Salmela-Aro, 2016; Marshall & Butler, 2016). This chapter will review evidence of maturation through connections with social institutions within two domains: Employment (as a part of adult social role maturation) and civic/communal maturation. Society, and a young person's role within it, plays an important role in facilitating maturation and desistance.

DOI: 10.4324/9781003143581-7

Employment

Employment plays a significant role as a turning point for young people progressing through the life course. Criminologists have found consistent evidence for employment supporting the desistance processes of young people (e.g., Horney et al., 1995; Laub & Sampson, 2003; Sampson & Laub, 1993). Traditionally, theory and research within criminology have considered this employment in a binary fashion: does one have a job? Many criminologists have expanded this conceptualization and operationalization to consider the quality and quantity of work. This extension includes factors that affect variability in job achievement, such as number of hours employed, job type, degrees earned, or salary. Largely, these theorizations of employment have been economically grounded in that having a job where one makes a sufficient salary or spends a significant portion of their day provides a turning point out of crime, or a reason to stay away from deviance. The risk of losing the job threatens one's livelihood and most deviance is not worth this risk to young people.

Emerging adulthood theory argues that the role of employment in the life course has shifted in line with structural changes in society. For Millennials and Generation Z, the workplace offers an opportunity for self-expression, fulfillment, and enjoyment (Arnett, 2004). This perspective toward employment is a distinct contrast to the approach of earlier generations, who accepted that while employment may be unpleasant, its main function was to earn a living (Arnett, 2004, 2015). This change is attributed to structural shifts in society regarding work including what it takes to get work (e.g., training, education), what work means to one's identity (e.g., having a fulfilling, satisfying, or meaningful job), and environmental barriers to achieving work (e.g., job market, economic stability; Côté & Bynner, 2008; Salvatore & Taniguchi, 2012).

First, the entry-level workforce has shifted compared to previous generations. With the continued advancement of society, and considering the emphasis on technological advancements, the amount of training and education required to earn an entry-level position has escalated. In particular, the emphasis on education has been culturally pervasive, with college often being utilized as an opportunity to explore different areas of study and consider potential occupational trajectories (Arnett, 2000; Magolda & Taylor, 2016; Marshall & Butler, 2016). Trends in both high school and college degree completion have continued to rise steadily since the mid-1900s (see Figure 6.1). When, for example, Sampson and Laub studied turning points in the early 1990s, the US population of adults aged 25 years or older had a rate of around 75% for high school graduates and approximately 20% for earning a bachelor's degree. In 2021, these rates have risen among this population to around 91% for high school graduates and 38% for earning a bachelor's degree.

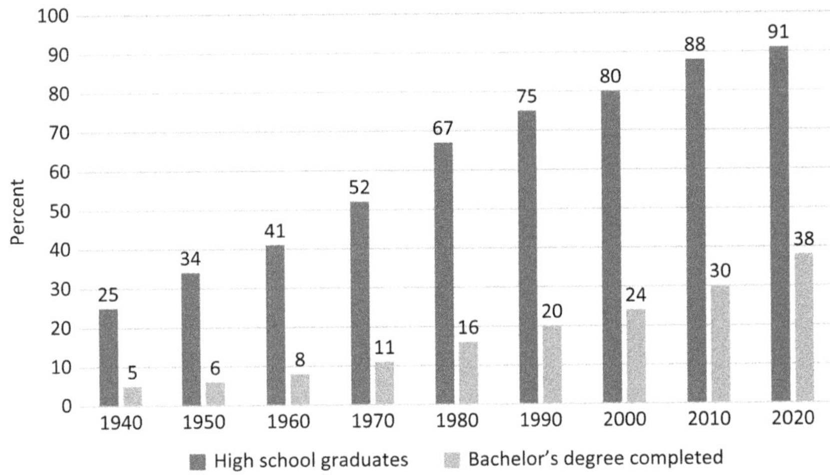

FIGURE 6.1 Percent of Population 25 Years and over Who Have Completed High School or College: 1940–2020. Source: US Census Bureau Report Number C2KBR-24 and Press Release Number CB22-TPS.02.

In addition to this shift in degree qualifications, the meaning of a job has altered as well. For many young people, selecting a field of employment or employer is more than securing a paycheck. Cultural shifts have placed an emphasis on having fulfilling and meaningful work for young people. One's career can serve as an important investment in one's identity, maturation, and quality of life (Arnett, 2000; Dietrich & Salmela-Aro, 2016; Marshall & Butler, 2016). This shift has major implications for criminology, and for those involved in the justice system. As young people coming out of the justice system often face barriers in accessing work overall, the implication of this may be amplified when meaningful or fulfilling work cannot be secured.

For example, consider a young person required to get a job as a part of their probation conditions. They may be able to secure a job in the service industry or in a warehouse packing boxes to be shipped. A probation officer may check in on how work is going to ensure that they remain employed and consider this sufficient – and certainly many criminologists would operationalize employment as such in their quantitative models. However, what would be the longer-term effects of this situation for an emerging adult? This type of work may be sufficient for some young people, but emerging adult theory tells us it is not sufficient for the majority of Millennials and Generation Z. By not being able to establish a career they find fulfilling and satisfying, young people are stunted in their progress toward seeing themselves as an adult. They may view themselves as still in a temporary job, a temporary place that they don't have to truly invest their energy into (Arnett, 2000; Dietrich & Salmela-Aro, 2016).

This effect is amplified for justice-involved emerging adults who face barriers in achieving adulthood markers (Fader, 2013; King et al., 2007; Schiraldi et al., 2015; Uggen et al., 2004; Uggen & Wakefield, 2005; Wakefield & Apel, 2016; Western, 2006). When other adulthood markers or roles cannot be achieved, they may rely on work as a primary turning point for desistance. If these justice-involved emerging adults get stuck in positions they do not want to be in, this could amplify the impulsivity indicative of emerging adulthood. This may make emerging adults more likely to engage in risky behaviors (e.g., drug use, crime, deviance) because they do not feel as if they have much at stake with this type of employment.

Therefore, for the emerging adult, all employment is not perceived as equal. This changes the conceptualization and operationalization of employment as a turning point from classical criminological theory. Researchers must begin to address and measure these additional facets of employment to fully understand if it is functioning as a turning point, and in what capacity, for emerging adults. This remains necessary to facilitate revisions to theory and research, as well as to inform how policy and practice can be developed to support young people attempting to desist in accessing education and employment that can facilitate desistance.

Participants in this study acknowledged that their transition out of risky, deviant, and/or criminal behaviors is necessary for them to embrace a prosocial future in line with societal norms and values indicative of adulthood. These norms and values, such as establishing a career or securing financial stability, are directly tied to their actions within society. Thus, these commitments set the stage for how participants engage in prosocial involvements. This was especially evident in narratives about establishing a career and/or pursuing an education.

For many participants, commitment to engaging in societal norms through a career was not difficult to imagine. Kareem provides an apropos example of this. When asked to describe what the next chapter in his life would be, Kareem, who has frequently taken jobs as a lifeguard, responded:

Kareem: That's easy. I'm trying to be a paramedic. I'm still trying to save lives. I'm just trying to advance now into a higher role.

Interviewer: You talked a little bit about that before, but what is it about being a paramedic specifically that appeals to you? Why did you decide about this field? What is drawing you into it?

Kareem: What draw me into it is because it's like I'm always helping people out, anybody who has come up to me for advice, some people come up to me for support on what to do next or something like that. Me being a lifeguard too is making me realize, damn, I keep saving lives. I want to take this higher. I want to be out there 24/7. I have so much energy that I feel I can fit there. I don't know, I just thought one day to myself, I'm just trying to be a paramedic, something new. Nobody in my family's a paramedic. I don't know, just a new role.

In addition to identifying a career, Kareem expresses the importance of engaging in caregiving through this career. By being a lifeguard, he realizes that he can care for others through a meaningful job while also providing a service to society and his community. He wants to further this connection to his community through his career by becoming a paramedic. This job would allow him to transition into a prosocial adulthood role while continuing to engage in the identity transformation process he is currently undertaking in his meaningful work as a lifeguard.

Employment through the Community-Based Organization

The participants in this study were all actively engaged in a community-based organization, which provided structured employment, education, and recreational activities during the weekdays. The community-based organization offers several areas of employment that young people can switch between during their time enrolled in the organization, such as food service, carpentry, and labor work. Each of these areas has several types of positions available. For example, in food service, they can work as kitchen staff, as a cashier, as a server, or in events and catering. Additional programming includes GED courses, introductory college-level courses, fitness programs, and other activities like book club, art classes, and access to a multimedia recording studio. These activities and programs mimic those that many other adolescents or emerging adults may experience while enrolled in college or in a vocational program, but with a focus on serving those with histories of justice-system involvement.

The majority of participants discussed how their ability to get work experience, training, and education (including their GED [General Educational Development certificate] or high school degree equivalent) was integral to their continued involvement in the community-based organization. For many of these young people, their efforts to seek employment or enroll in school were impeded by their justice-system involvement. The organization, however, offered assistance in overcoming structural barriers they otherwise felt they could not overcome on their own. Desistance, thus, remains a driving theme for young people and their choice to engage in the organization.

Again, participation in this community-based organization is completely voluntary for these young people. None of them are assigned here as a condition of probation or parole, although many corrections officers certainly support recruitment into the organization. Participants recognized that their continued engagement is voluntary, but their commitment to their own transformation and maturation motivates them to keep attending. The community-based organization offers a key type of support for justice-involved young people trying to engage in this type of identity transformation. Daniel expressed this clearly in his narrative:

> They open a lot of doors for you. It's only if you give your 100% in there, like coming every day, doing the work, progressing forward. If you come in and you just chill, to see your friends, don't really take it serious, you're just going to be stuck. Basically. That's why I want to come here, show them that I'm interested, I care, I want this, and see where the open doors lead me.

Participants generally perceive the community-based organization as providing opportunities they otherwise could not have accessed. It provides support for a pathway into desistance while gaining work experience, education, and training – meeting many of the needs of these young people working to establish their roles in society. This put many of the participants in a place where they were able to explore various adult roles under the purview of a social institution.

Daniel also emphasizes something important in stating that young people need to give their "100% in there". A young person's own agency plays a vital part in the desistance process. Engagement in the program can be effective in supporting desistance and the transition to adulthood for those employing agentic activity, as discussed in Chapter 2. It is not too far of a stretch to compare this with the experience of college, where young people must also work hard to pass their classes, get an internship or work experience, and eventually find a job in their field of study. Emerging adults in college certainly have just as much opportunity to "come in", "just chill", and have fun with their friends without employing the agentic activity necessary to mature in their adult role of the career.

Daniel's quote, however, is not meant to dismiss the role of social support in the context of seeking employment as an adult role. Certainly, the social context of this community-based organization affects one's agentic activity within it. Participants in this study emphasized that feelings of support and togetherness they experienced while participating with the community-based organization were central to their commitment to the organization. They also placed value on the relationships they formed with other young people engaged in the organization. Participants strongly emphasized that the community-based organization provided many of these young people with a more enjoyable and meaningful experience than working other jobs or attending GED courses independently. Several of the participants even compared their engagement with the organization as being their version of college, underlining that their experiences were putting them onto a developmental trajectory equivalent to that of their non-justice-involved peers.

When asked why she keeps coming back to the organization, Emma says

> The positive energy. Nobody likes to go to a job they hate. So, they make it a good place to be. I feel like they're going to help me in life.

She acknowledges that in addition to the support she receives, the atmosphere of the organization provides additional motivation to continue her involvement. This ties back to the goal emerging adults have for establishing satisfying and meaningful work. Additionally, the support that she receives reflects the value emerging adults place on what makes relationships with social institutions so important. For Emma, the organization provides this opportunity for satisfying and meaningful work while surrounded by peers and mentors that she can trust.

Meaningful Work

Establishing a career that they found enjoyable, meaningful, and/or satisfying was one of the central themes for participant narratives of desistance. This is directly in line with theorizations under the emerging adult perspective (Arnett, 2004) as well as criminological perspectives toward maturation and desistance (Rocque, 2015). Carlos expresses this with his goal of becoming an emergency medical technician (EMT) here:

> I really want to be an EMT. I know they don't make money like that, but that's something exciting and I want to do something that I love. You know what I'm saying? I don't want to have a job where I'm just like, damn, I don't even want to go in, and then be miserable the whole day. It's terrible. Because I've dealt with it. I just feel whatever makes me happy in the end and if there's money in my pockets, and my son's all right, then what could be worse? You know what I'm saying?

Carlos highlights something important here indicative of the perspective of emerging adults by saying that he knows EMTs "don't make money like that". Here, he is acknowledging that he is not thinking about or selecting his career based on the pay. Instead, he emphasizes that he wants a job that is exciting and enjoyable, and one where he can potentially make a contribution to society. Participants generally recognized that their commitment to establishing a career does not have to mean settling for a job they do not want or enjoy.

Participants also acknowledged their paths in attempting to achieve this goal of establishing meaningful and satisfying employment may not be quick or easy. For example, Zoe identifies wanting to become a police officer and discusses her path into making this decision:

> So I want to study criminal justice. Yeah, and I'm excited for it. I've put it off, not because I had a kid, or not because of all the obstacles. I literally waited for a reason. I've seen so many people start [college], leave, start, leave, owe debt. I mean, of course there were a few people who started and finished, four years. They banged it out. But I know that that wouldn't have worked for me. School was never for me. I hated it, and now that I see the purpose in it, it's clear. I wanted to be so many things. I wanted to be a counselor. I wanted to be a firewoman. I wanted to be so many things, but now I finally, like for a good year it hasn't changed, or I haven't had to question what I wanted to be. I figure it'll take me a good amount of time to become a policewoman, you know, with the school, and then you have to go to the police academy and all that. Figure it'll take me at least four to six years, if not eight years until I get that goal.

Here, Zoe understands that this process of establishing a satisfying and meaningful career is not one of instant gratification. Although she has not tried out these various careers of being a counselor or firewoman, she acknowledges that she did consider seriously what it would take to achieve these goals. Zoe is recognizing here that she is exploring her career options through important self-reflection, self-assessment, and meaning making for her future. By emphasizing that she has not had to question becoming a policewoman for the past year, Zoe is acknowledging that this exploration process is coming to a close and she outlines her plan to begin the trajectory toward achieving this career goal.

In addition, Zoe highlights how her need to find enjoyable work may compound upon other factors one considers when choosing employment. Here, she discusses how she quit a job that involved a long commute which made it difficult for her to balance other responsibilities in her life, such as parenting:

> So this Summer I quit a good job I had, because I don't know, I guess I was in a good point at that point. I thought a new job would come. It was a far commute, so I was like, "I'm done with that." It was a stressful ... I didn't really like the job, either. But shortly after, I couldn't find a job that I wanted. I didn't want to work at [a fast food restaurant] or anything like that. So I couldn't find a job. I ended up losing my car, because I couldn't pay my insurance, then the registration went, and everything was going downhill, literally, until recently when I came to [the community-based organization]. I started working. It worked out on my schedule. I was able to save money. And now I have my car back on the road. I have my own apartment. Everything's going good. So that's the turning point for me.

Zoe explains that when she quit her job, she did not want to take another job that she did not find enjoyable. Although she acknowledges that she did need a job and recognizes the consequences of being unemployed, which included losing her car, she still emphasizes the value of finding enjoyable work. Zoe identifies that finding enjoyable work at the community-based organization, where she can also earn a stable paycheck and balance her other responsibilities, functioned as a turning point into adulthood. Through this employment, Zoe sees herself as making progress in her career and successfully moving toward the adult role of a stable career.

Several participants expressed that furthering their work experience, education, or training was an important aspect of success in establishing a meaningful career. For example, after his most recent release from jail, Bruno discussed seeking out workforce training programs to help him secure stable employment. Upon his release, he applied to a local workforce training program. While there, he was able to go through OSHA (Occupational Safety and Health Administration) training as well as ServSafe, a food and beverage safety training and certification program:

> I get out and I go to this program … So, what I did with them was, got my OSHA, got my ServSafe certificate with them. And then they would take us out on job sites, construction sites, and teach us how to do or not even teach us, that's what we had to do the OSHA for. We would have to build sheds. They would let us get the hands-on experience of a construction worker, and then we would get paid every two weeks for coming.

For Bruno, engaging in these trainings and earning certificates served as justification he could utilize for future employers who may be wary of hiring someone with a criminal record. Through furthering their experience, education, or training, justice-involved emerging adults earn additional qualifications that can help in the employment-seeking process. Additionally, for participants in this study, these qualifications may help them overcome the barriers of their justice involvement (i.e., criminal record).

For emerging adults, the concept of employment stretches beyond earning a paycheck, indicating a shift from many classical operationalizations of criminological theory. Justice-involved emerging adults in this sample were dedicated to finding work that was both satisfying and enjoyable, which is characteristic of emerging adulthood. Emerging adults view their career as an opportunity for fulfillment and enjoyment, which is distinct from earlier generations that approach employment as an unpleasant necessity (Arnett, 2004, 2015). Establishing enjoyable employment may thus support the desistance from crime within the transition to adulthood.

Career Exploration

Finally, participants valued the opportunity for career exploration, which is typical for emerging adults (e.g., Arnett, 2000; Dietrich & Salmela-Aro, 2016; Marshall & Butler, 2016). Tiffany, for example, identified that she enjoys being able to try new jobs within the community-based organization.

> If I work at [a coffee shop], I will literally work there for a month and then I'll get bored and I'll quit my job. Or I'll go in healthcare and I'll work there for two months or three months and then I'll get bored and I'll quit my job. And [this community-based organization] is a place where even if you do get bored, you just switch your department, so you're not really quitting your job.

For Tiffany, these positions may serve to mimic the experience of an apprenticeship or internship, where people can spend time working in a field or with a company to gain skills and learn about an industry before committing to a finalized career. It is important to highlight here that the community-based organization serves to compensate for the impulsivity in quitting jobs Tiffany and other young people have not enjoyed. This type of impulsivity is characteristic of emerging adulthood, as emerging adults are not yet tied to their career roles and instead embrace this type of exploration and change.

This community-based organization, therefore, affords the opportunity for justice-involved emerging adults to embrace the exploration of different work environments and tasks while maintaining the stability of remaining employed. This is especially important for emerging adults like Tiffany who also face the challenge of applying for jobs with a criminal record, as employers may not desire interviewing or hiring someone with a criminal record (Pager, 2003; Pager et al., 2009; Uggen et al., 2014). She continues to describe how the community-based organization is more enjoyable than other jobs she has held:

> I feel like [the community-based organization] puts you in a position where you kind of like working because you're always talking and hanging out with other people and communicating. So it's not really like, oh, you have to work, work, work. You know what I mean? So you have that flexibility. Rather than being in a real job and you're miserable the whole time.

This emphasis on enjoyment while working highlights how employment may not function for justice-involved emerging adults as previously conceptualized with other samples (e.g., Maruna, 2001; Sampson & Laub, 1993). This may be exacerbated by the instability of emerging adulthood where it is typical for young people to explore various work roles (Arnett, 2000; Dietrich & Salmela-Aro, 2016; Marshall & Butler, 2016). This role exploration may facilitate impulsivity to change or quit jobs frequently when emerging adults do not find them enjoyable or fulfilling just as Tiffany did. Emerging adults may do this more frequently than people in other developmental phases in order to meet the needs of finding satisfying and meaningful (Arnett, 2004, 2015).

Civic/Communal Maturation

Civic or communal maturation is conceptualized through the actions of young people who contribute to being a good citizen of society. Theoretically, citizenship and civic engagement have been proposed as key components of prosocial development among young people (Balsano, 2005). This domain also includes volunteer work or community work, voting or political involvement, and financial contributions (e.g., paying taxes, making donations). Citizenship and civic engagement thus represent one's belief in the common values of society. Through their behaviors and involvements, young people can demonstrate their prosocial maturation through the adherence to these values (Flanagan & Levine, 2010).

Criminologists have long acknowledged the importance of a commitment to civic engagement (e.g., *collective efficacy*, Sampson et al., 1997; the *belief* component of social bond theory, Hirschi, 1969) in preventing deviance and/or promoting desistance. Generativity is one concept that captures this, as it allows those embracing or entering adulthood to engage in contributing to the larger sphere of society by shifting their perspective away from their own needs and toward identifying how they can support others around them (see Erikson, 1950, 1963; see also Maruna, 2001; McAdams & de St. Aubin, 1992; McAdams et al., 1998).

Participation in one's community provides an important mechanism for young people to establish a prosocial role in that community (Uggen & Janikula, 1999; Uggen et al., 2004). Young people with criminal records, however, may face barriers in their efforts to engage in citizenship within their communities (Manza & Uggen, 2004, 2008; Uggen & Manza, 2005). Often, these young people will need additional support to regain this access to civic engagement in line with their peers who are not entangled in the justice system. This support may, and often does, come from community-based organizations that serve justice-involved young people (Fox, 2015, 2016; Nader, 2019).

During their interviews, participants were asked to describe the expected behaviors of community members, including those of "good" community members, and if their own behaviors were influenced by meeting these criteria. Participants generally shared a common view that being a community member is grounded in giving back, helping, or supporting others in the community.

Participants often identified concepts of collective efficacy, including social cohesion and providing support (Sampson et al., 1997), as being central to the responsibilities of community members. Thus, it stands that these emerging adults do believe that common values exist within their communities and that these societal values are acceptable and fair.

One participant, Emma, simply stated that good community members "will treat everybody equal". Here, she acknowledges that the fairness of the values of society is the most important part of this component. For Emma, the common values of a community are related to how people treat each other on a daily basis and the consistency in distributing this treatment. This is reflective of the norms associated with the transition into adulthood and embracement of generativity through modeling behavior based on societal expectations (see Erikson, 1950, 1963; see also Maruna, 2001; McAdams & de St. Aubin, 1992; McAdams et al., 1998).

Participants also provided examples of both small and large gestures of community members giving back. Through this process of giving back, emerging adults can contribute to society while embracing their own transitions into adulthood as outlined through the theme of generativity. For example, Diego emphasizes that good community members should:

> Just like give back. You can give back in all types of ways, or you can even just say hi, just even say hi to the poor people. Or just don't be like ... I don't really know how to explain it. It's just a whole bunch of different ways you can be good to the community, you know what I mean. Yesterday, we closed down the café every Thursday, we don't open Fridays, so all the food, we throw it away. What me and [a coworker], what we going to start doing is all the food that we throw away we're going to take to a shelter. We start doing that yesterday, ain't nobody tell us to do that we just thought about it ourselves. That's one way you can be good in the community, and you're not even doing much for too much people, you're just giving out stuff that you're going to throw away. That's just like an example.

Here, Diego provides examples of social cohesion through smaller gestures such as saying hi to people as well larger gestures such as supporting community members by donating food to shelters.

Carlos echoes this theme by describing the importance of supporting one's neighbors:

> Give a helping hand. It's really basic manners, you know? And common courtesy. You gotta understand if you was in that position, if you wanted help would you get it or not? So you gotta be that person to step over the line, and stand up. You know what I'm saying?

Here, Carlos is acknowledging that helping neighbors is at the base of his belief of what community members are supposed to do. Respect and reciprocity are among the core values of what defines a community for Carlos. The social cohesion among neighbors who share values is central to how participants view communities.

Bruno provides another example in his description of a neighbor he thinks emulates the concept of community:

> I had this neighbor that used to wake up all the time, faithfully every day. He used to just watch people walk by and he used to clean everybody's little sidewalk or in front of their house or whatever. He cleaned their steps, whatever. He always saying hi to everybody. Everybody knew him. He was just a kind person. I feel like that's the kind of people we need, because he just was a positive person overall. He may have had his own little problems or whatever, but he didn't let nobody see that. He just stayed positive in all his situations, and he just good morning to everybody. Because, even little stuff like that, saying good morning to somebody, could actually change their whole mood for a day or for that day, and it could uplift them, you know what I mean? Little stuff like that. He was that guy. He used to just talk to everybody, it didn't matter who it was.

Bruno recognizes that although this neighbor may have had his own problems in life, he remained friendly and supportive to others in his community. Thus, he identifies this neighbor as prime example of where he learned about the values of community, highlighting that through generativity, adults can contribute to society by modeling behaviors for others (Erikson, 1950, 1963; Maruna, 2001; McAdams & de St. Aubin, 1992; McAdams et al., 1998).

Contributing to keeping the community clean persisted as an important common behavior for community members. When expressing what good community members are supposed to do, Dylan says, "Help other people. Not litter. That's pretty big". Likewise, Tiffany echoes this:

> Just like looking after your community. If you see somebody doing something wrong, say something. Caring about your community, not dirtying your community, keeping your community clean.

Keeping the community clean, including tasks such as caring for sidewalks and picking up trash, is viewed as a part of taking care of the community. Thus, these participants view this type of care as central to the common values of community members.

Political Engagement

Participants also discussed the importance of getting involved with local politics, including voting. Sebastian discusses that he learned from other members of the community-based organization the importance of voting. Now, Sebastian engages in voting for every election, from "little city council" to "congress":

> Whatever type of election, I was looking up, trying to find out as much information as possible on the candidate. Why? Because I know that person's about to be in the city… running the community, our community.

A few of the participants took this engagement a step further as a part of a group organizing for criminal justice reform. This organizing included many other youths from the community-based organization in tandem with the community overall. In their work, they advocated in support of reforms for the juvenile justice system, including bills targeting the expungement of juvenile criminal records and raising the age of purview of the juvenile justice system to 21. This included young people traveling to the state legislature to share their own stories of justice-system involvement.

One of these participants, Kareem, echoed the importance of this after one of the bills they were promoting passed a vote in the State House: "That's something exciting in my life that I feel like I did something for the community, people like me". He continues to discuss the personal importance of these efforts for himself, and others like him, in removing some of the barriers young people face via criminal justice reform and civic engagement. This type of work is something that, as he says, "keeps popping up into my head" and he sees this kind of work as important. For Kareem, if his record becomes expunged, he can:

> be clean… [and] could do my stuff now. That's something good that I did for not just me but everybody else that has criminal records like me

Kareem also recognizes that this type of involvement is one that can help shift how others perceive him. During his interview, he reflected on how friends and acquaintances began reaching out and acknowledging him after they saw him on the local news and in newspapers:

> People that I know that be like, "Hey, look, you're on the news. Look at, your name is out there." Because I've been on newspapers and stuff like that, so people see that stuff, and they be like, "Look, you're in the newspaper." They notice things. I feel like they see like, damn, he's changing not for himself but to try to help. I feel like that's the way I want to be recognized is like, he was a helper.

For Kareem, this recognition played an important role in reinforcing that he was getting "on track" and in line with expectations from his community. Although this did not motivate his initial involvement in this civic engagement, it served as positive reinforcement for Kareem to continue engaging in this effort. He acknowledged that this was important for his own identity change in that he can now been seen by others as a "helper", allowing him to embrace a redemption narrative among both close friends and acquaintances.

Interestingly, although participants acknowledge that they do recognize the importance of civic engagement, and while they may even engage in it, they may not directly connect this to their own adult identities. Although participants seem to have a similar view on the expected behavior of the community members, they did not believe that this directly influenced their own desistance, other than the example above provided by Kareem about being seen in the local news as a form of positive reinforcement. When prompted to explain why, participants expressed that behaviors of civic engagement and those of a "good" community member would be important when they achieve a "full" adulthood.

This, in part, may be attributed to the socio-structural shifts of society by which the common values of society, and contribution to it via civic engagement, may not be as crucial for emerging adults as theorized for adolescents or for previous generations of young people (Arnett, 2000; Elder, 1998; Sampson & Laub, 1993). This is in line with findings from the work of Rocque and colleagues (2015), where in their test of maturation, they found that young people did not exhibit an increase in civic maturation during the transition from adolescence into young adulthood. In turn, civic maturation was thus not influential on measures of crime in either the between- or within-individual domains.

Therefore, civic or communal engagements may be perceived by emerging adults as exploratory, just as they view social engagements in other facets of their lives – like romantic relationships or careers. Emerging adulthood may provide these young people with an opportunity to explore if and how they want to engage civically. These findings may be considered a challenge to the mechanism of civic engagement for facilitating an identity shift for emerging adults. While young people may not internalize these behaviors of civic engagement into their own maturing identities, this does not preclude others from recognizing them as such. Their behaviors as a community member may still influence how others in their social networks (e.g., parents, friends, criminal justice officials) perceive them and their maturation, emphasizing the social implications of this maturation domain.

Conclusion

Social institutions and a young person's connections to them play an important role in the maturation process. Emerging adulthood is a life stage where young people are experimenting with their perspectives toward and involvement in social institutions. The context of these social institutions has also shifted from previous generations, where emerging adults prioritize this exploration later into the life course than previous generations. They also emphasize the need to have meaningful, fulfilling, and satisfying engagements in these social institutions. If encounters with social institutions, such as employment or civic engagement, do not meet these needs, it threatens if and how these function as turning points. This has important implications for the desistance process and turning points out of crime.

An important change of context within social institutions for emerging adults focuses on employment. In the study of desistance, criminologists traditionally theorize and operationalize employment in an economical sense – considering if one has a job or defining the quality of a job by factors such as the number of hours employed or salary. Emerging adulthood theory argues that the most important factors of employment center around the meaningfulness and enjoyment of the work. Employment, thus, shifts from a monetarily driven social institution to one where young people yearn to present their identities to themselves and others. This has important implications for desistance, as young people may not view jobs as permanent or important unless they meet these goals of creating meaning and fulfillment. Instead, young people who are in jobs they view as temporary may be less likely to use these positions as a turning point out of crime.

Participants in this sample and their perspectives were certainly in line with the propositions of emerging adulthood theory. For participants, even though they understood the necessity of work, and the limitations on their access to work and education as a result of their justice-system involvement, they still had notable goals for their working adult self. Importantly, these young people emphasized that they wanted a chance to explore various types of careers or engage in training and education to learn more about their desired fields of employment. Ultimately, these participants emphasized that they wanted to work in a position that was enjoyable and meaningful to them. For these young people, this was the marker of success in both maturation and desistance.

Maturation across the domain of civic or communal engagement is also important to examine within the desistance process. Across many variations of theory, criminologists account for the role of civic engagement in desistance or in promoting adherence to prosocial norms. Participation in one's community is an opportunity for young people to embrace the values of their communities and social institutions. Certainly, participants in this sample understood the values of their communities and what makes a "good" member of the community. These participants even began to engage in these behaviors as a part of their desistance processes. Intriguingly, participants did not connect this civic engagement as central to their maturation processes. Instead, participants saw being a "good" member of the community as something they should strive for after they had reached maturation into adulthood. This phase in the life course may thus provide young people with an opportunity to explore civic engagement. Similar to other turning points, emerging adulthood is a time where young people can determine what kind of civically engaged adult they want to be for their community. This, in turn, may affect if and how civic engagement can function within an individual's desistance process as a turning point out of crime.

7

IMPLICATIONS FOR POLICY AND PRACTICE

Throughout this book, I explored the theorization of turning points and maturation of young and emerging adults engaging in desistance. Largely, the focus of this text is to provide an interdisciplinary approach to understanding desistance for emerging adults, merging evidence from the fields of criminology, sociology, and developmental psychology with my own findings. Through my narrative interviews with justice-involved emerging adults, I worked to understand how cognitive, social, and structural factors influence the desistance process within emerging adulthood. This allowed me to examine how today's justice-involved emerging adult engages in the transition to adulthood, including the transformation of their identities and how they embrace turning points into adult roles. Ultimately, this research provides evidence to assist in improving the conceptualization and operationalization of desistance within the life course for justice-involved emerging adults.

Importantly though, I cannot end this book without discussing the impacts of this work across the domains of policy and practice. By working to extend theorizations, implications to policy naturally arise that can help shape how the justice system works to address the needs of younger adults engaging in desistance and reentry. In this final chapter, I work through the conclusions of my research and its potential implications for policy. I organized this across the two overarching maturation domains dissected in this book: psychological maturation and social maturation. The conclusions and the recommendations presented build on each other as the chapter progresses, reflecting the interwoven nature of the domains of maturation.

As you read through this chapter, you may note that many of my recommendations focus on the system itself and not on the emerging adults. I direct these recommendations to practitioners, policy makers, scholars, and

DOI: 10.4324/9781003143581-8

activists who work in and around the justice system. My perspective is as such because I interpret the evidence in the fields of emerging adulthood and criminology presented in this text as indicating that our social systems need to be adjusted to bend to the needs of today's young person.

Therefore, the inherent argument here is that there is not anything wrong with the young people involved in the justice system who are taking risks and working to discover "who they are". In fact, this is extremely age-appropriate. These young people do not necessarily need to "fix" themselves as they progress through their natural paths of maturity. Instead, the system that encompasses them has a responsibility to meet the needs of these young people in order to facilitate their development into prosocial adults. As a criminologist, I would compare many of these recommendations to the framework of rehabilitation encompassed traditionally in our juvenile justice system. Extending this type of support to emerging adults may provide justice-involved emerging adults with an opportunity to embrace maturation, allowing them to access turning points in line with their developmental needs of exploration in search of an identity project and supporting their desistance processes.

Psychological Maturation

Cognitive Transformation and Identity Maturation

Psychological maturation and cognitive development are integral to the process of growing up for young people, reflecting one's self-perceptions and attitudes toward society. Emerging adulthood is characterized as a period of instability, where young people explore the possibilities of who they are and what they want to do with their lives. As young people embrace psychological maturation, they can establish stability in their sense of self, helping them settle into their identities as adults and recognize their own maturity. This process is particularly important for justice-involved young people working on desistance, who can use this psychological maturation as a turning point in their narratives to separate their younger, immature selves from their current or future mature, law-abiding selves.

Participants in this study echoed the importance of identity projects to their maturation processes. For these young people, identity projects offered "hooks" for change, affording them a path to "get on track" with their peers (Giordano et al., 2002; Maruna, 2001). Participants expressed two components that facilitated their own maturation and desistance process. First, participants recognized that they needed to embrace the concept of growing up. Delineating their past younger self from their current or future self was central to both maturation and desistance. Recognizing their own growth is central to the desistance process for these justice-involved emerging adults. Through the natural process of maturation, they can embrace the possibility that they were allowed to have made mistakes in the past as young, immature adolescents. By emerging into adulthood, they could prove that these mistakes do not define "who they are", especially in that they were not required to be labeled as delinquents or criminals for the rest of their lives. Instead, these young people could embrace the opportunity for redemption through maturation and identity change.

The second component requires an identity project (or projects) to latch onto. Participants in this sample had a variety of these projects, such as being a parent, which provided them with the blueprint for psychological maturation. Through their identity projects, participants embraced changes in their self-perceptions as well as their attitudes toward social institutions. For example, when participants were able to plan out their future career goals, they recognized the value of education in this process. For this sample, changes in attitudes toward deviance were some of the most pertinent, as these reflect their own desistance processes. Identity projects provided pathways through which they felt they could change their attitudes toward deviance, facilitating the desistance process alongside maturation.

Importantly, emerging adults need support in finding and establishing identity projects. Society is structured to provide adolescents with support systems through social institutions, such as the requirements of living with parents and attending school. Emerging adults, however, have no such requirements. The average emerging adult accesses this support through social institutions such as college or employment. Emerging adults can explore their options for identity projects in search of "who they are' through connections with peers, student organizations, local communities, professors, internships, or jobs. When emerging adults cannot access support for exploring their identities, this may place them on either an expedited or delayed path to adulthood (DeLuca et al., 2016; Halsey & Deegan, 2015; Salvatore, 2017; Salvatore et al., 2012). These expedited or delayed paths may threaten the function of identity projects as turning points in the desistance process.

Justice-involved emerging adults are likely to be disconnected from social institutions that can support their identity exploration. Yet, establishing identity projects is an integral part of desistance. Therefore, the criminal justice system and its stakeholders must work to develop structures that connect young people to social institutions that support the development of identity projects. The criminal justice system needs to adapt to serve young people in exploring and establishing identity projects in order to ensure their success in desistance during incarceration, reentry, and/or diversion.

Across the United States, we are starting to see examples of shifts in policies and practices aimed at targeting the needs of justice-involved emerging adults. This includes laws that increase the age of entry into the adult legal system and the creation of specialty services (i.e., courts, probation programs) directed at young and emerging adults. One of the most common changes in practice over the past few years has been the development of specialty courts focusing on young adults between the ages of approximately 18 and 25. These have been implemented in cities like Chicago,[1] San Francisco,[2] and New York.[3] These courts offer specialty interventions for young people that are not typical for the adult court system but that work to support these young people in their maturation process. These include access to alternatives to incarceration or diversion programming, reduced fees, record expungement, and access to social services.

There have also been shifts in the approaches of correctional institutions and community corrections that serve emerging adults. For example, some adult jails and prisons have begun to implement units focused on housing young adults, such as those in Connecticut[4] and Massachusetts.[5] These units provide resources specific to the needs of emerging adults, including access to education, promoting positive relationships both inside and outside of the institution, and support for psychological maturation (i.e., personal growth, socioemotional growth). Similar changes have been implemented in probation and parole departments, including in cities such as San Francisco,[6] Boston,[7] and as diversion programs, like in Austin[8] and Kalamazoo.[9] These changes to community corrections reflect the recognition of the unique needs of emerging adults entangled in the justice system.

In the case of participants in this study, they were able to access a local community-based intervention that served justice-involved young people. Through this organization, they were encouraged to explore various identity projects and provided with the support (materially and emotionally) to do so. Community-based interventions such as these may be integral to filling the gap of unique needs of justice-involved emerging adults (Salvatore & Taniguchi, 2012; Schiraldi et al., 2015). This may be especially important in communities where formal services like emerging adult courts have yet to be established.

Community-based organizations like this offer young people an opportunity to engage in desistance work that is in line with the needs of emerging adulthood. They can provide them with the resources to explore careers, promote prosocial relationships, establish stability, and shift attitudes toward one's self and one's community. These organizations can help to support emerging adults simultaneously working on maturation and desistance. They do so by targeting the key needs of emerging adults, including in promoting prosocial relationships and support networks with peers and families, improving health and well-being including socioemotional competence, and helping young people explore careers and education while establishing stability and financial security. Many of these organizations focus already on emerging adults, including in New York City,[10] Boston,[11] Baltimore,[12] and Lowell.[13]

While the participants in this study engaged with the community-based intervention voluntarily, many were connected by or encouraged to access services by criminal justice officials, including judges, probation and parole officers, and law enforcement. When possible, criminal justice officials should support emerging adults' access to these types of community-based interventions (Sakala et al., 2020). Importantly, these services do not exist in many communities and often are not ingrained in structures of the justice system such as correctional institutions. For the case of this study, this intervention was one that was located in an urban area and had close relationships with local law enforcement and corrections agencies. In addition, they had staff dedicated to seeking grant funding and fundraising in order to support the organization and the needs of the emerging adults. While many communities may not have organizations like this, they can access the work of organizations like this one and those mentioned above as models for developing new interventions to serve these youth. This will likely be an endeavor requiring the collaboration of city or public officials, community members, researchers, and activists to build successful community-based interventions.

Psychosocial Maturation

Psychosocial maturation works in tandem with cognitive transformation and identity maturation to provide young people with the opportunity to embrace their processes of growing up across the life course. This domain reflects a person's adaptive functioning and socioemotional competence, including one's development across components like autonomy, interpersonal skills, and social responsibility. Psychosocial maturation has particular importance for young people engaged in crime, as maturation in this domain is indicative of desistance. By recognizing that they are in control of their own behaviors and decisions, young people can take responsibility for their outcomes. Participants in this sample demonstrated their psychosocial maturation across three traditional domains: temperance, responsibility, and perspective.

First, the domain of temperance includes one's ability to limit impulsivity or aggression in favor of rational decision-making and acts of self-control. Participants in this sample shared specific examples of their own temperance within their desistance narratives, including instances where they were able to exhibit self-control or limit aggressive responses. These examples were important evidence for participants to recognize that they were maturing. This emphasized the role of temperance in self-perceptions of maturation while also displaying this maturation in social contexts, such as with a group of peers.

The second domain of responsibility represents one's autonomy. Participants in this sample typically demonstrated their own efforts toward autonomy through financial security. This is in line with how emerging adulthood theory postulates the importance of autonomy for this life stage. Participants recognized the importance of having a legitimate income source and a steady job as central to their process of maturation. By securing financial stability, participants could become autonomous and take on the responsibilities of adulthood for themselves (e.g., establishing housing, paying rent, and paying bills).

Third, the domain of perspective reflects one's consciousness and orientation toward their own future. Emerging adulthood is a period in the life course where young people are expected to build a plan for their futures. Participants in this sample did just that, providing evidence for their development of perspective within their maturation. Importantly, the components of this domain were intertwined with those of temperance and responsibility, emphasizing that perspective may be the culmination of (or subsequent to) maturation in the previous two domains. For example, participants often discussed wanting to build a family in the future. To do this, they recognized the importance of temperance and responsibility by acknowledging that they needed to do things like change their attitudes and establish financial security before they could begin to build a family.

Psychosocial maturation builds on the component of cognitive transformation and identity maturation by emphasizing psychological maturity in adaptive functioning and socioemotional competence. As the previous section's recommendations emphasized a need to connect justice-involved emerging adults with social institutions, this section's recommendations expand on this by providing direction for the types of services justice-involved emerging adults need from social institutions. For young people to progress on the path of maturation, they need to develop their adaptive functioning and socioemotional competence.

Theory, combined with the evidence presented here, suggests that when emerging adults can mature across the domains of temperance, responsibility, and perspective, they can embrace desistance. Interventions targeting emerging adults both in and around the criminal justice system need to emphasize these domains of psychological maturation in their programming. This may include creating new programming, or connecting to already existing programming, that aims to help emerging adults build skills under the domains of temperance, responsibility, and perspective. These include exercising self-control, building autonomy and financial stability, and creating a plan for the future. Programs that target factors like these can help justice-involved emerging adults overcome the barriers of their system involvement to mature in line with their peers while emphasizing desistance.

Social Maturation

Relationships and Social Support

Relationships are important to our social identities and our experiences with the world. They also offer an opportunity to reflect upon one's self and one's approach to the world. The contexts of a young person's relationships change as they age out of adolescence and into their late teens and early 20s, including both the expectations and needs of relationships. While the average emerging adult has access to social institutions that can support these changes, those entangled in the criminal justice system face barriers in accessing positive social relationships in line with this life stage. These barriers have important effects on constraining how young people can form or maintain the relationships they need to support both maturation and desistance.

When young people are incarcerated, they face some of the most pervasive barriers in accessing both preexisting prosocial relationships and forming new ones. They have limited access to seeing and speaking with people on the outside of these institutions. When they do get access, this access is typically restricted (i.e., restrictions on touching or times/lengths of visits) or placed behind a paywall (i.e., charges for phone and video calls). Together, these limit how young people can form or maintain the social support necessary for both maturation and desistance. Importantly, people out in the community do not face such harsh implications, magnifying the delays in maturation experienced by young people who are incarcerated.

One key shift emerging adults experience is in their relationship with their parents. Generally, emerging adults want to establish material independence from parents while increasing their emotional connection and reliance on parents (Copp et al., 2019; Dubas & Petersen, 1996; Giordano et al., 2007; Johnson et al., 2011; O'Connor et al., 1996). This is indicative of the maturation process and progression across the life course for young people. Justice-system involvement, however, poses a threat to this maturation. Young people who get entangled in the justice system will experience barriers, such as difficulty finding (well-paying) employment, that can inhibit success in establishing material independence. This may strain relationships between emerging adults and their parents as they continue their reliance on parents for housing and financial support, if they can offer it, well into emerging adulthood.

This compounds upon the expectations of relationships for emerging adults as they leave adolescence and the contexts of their relationships shift. Emerging adults begin to focus on building relationships centered on qualities such as trust and support, especially when these relationships support desistance. For emerging adults, friendships often become the primary social support, filling the gap created during identity exploration between the childhood family and establishing a family as an adult (Allan, 2008; Demir & Özdemir, 2010; Guan & Fuligni, 2016). Friends can thus often become the most important relationships for justice-involved emerging adults as they can support both identity change and desistance (Mawson et al., 2015). As a part of developing a prosocial support network, emerging adults who want to desist engage in a process of cutting criminogenic ties. In lieu of these social supports, they will need to build new prosocial ties and networks.

In response, the justice system must shift its approach to facilitating relationship building for emerging adults in order to support their desistance processes. First and foremost, this change must come with the accessibility to communication with support networks while incarcerated. Young people are limited in their access to the outside world while incarcerated. While this may be beneficial in limiting ties with criminogenic connections, it also has a detrimental effect on maintaining necessary prosocial relationships. Considering the advances in technology that exist, it would be easy for many institutions that already have access to technology (i.e., tablets, phones, computers) to set up conditions where people who are incarcerated can speak to prosocial ties, such as parents, more freely. In particular, these institutions need to move beyond paywalled structures of communication where those who are incarcerated are required to pay to communicate with the outside world. This will require the justice system to move away from partnerships with third-party companies that monetize the communications of incarcerated individuals, which some states have recently started to embrace like Connecticut[14] and California[15] in 2022. Limiting communication with key relationships, like parents, may threaten the success of young people who reenter into society after incarceration.

For justice-involved emerging adults who are either incarcerated or in the community, criminal justice practices must move toward emphasizing social support as a necessary part of rehabilitation and desistance. Emerging adults will likely not be able to desist without proper social support. In particular, the unique connections emerging adults seek with parents should be considered in the development of intervention for justice-involved emerging adults. This includes programming that can help promote healthy emotional relationships with parents and programming that can help emerging adults establish material independence (i.e., financial, housing) from parents.

The criminal justice system must also create programming, or connect young people with existing programming, that supports the development of other social relationships. In particular, emerging adults need to establish a close network of friends or peers they can rely on to support their own identity exploration, maturation, and desistance. This may include local organizations, such as recreational leagues, neighborhood associations, or community-based interventions like the one in this study. Connecting young people with programming specific to their needs or interests may be particularly beneficial. For example, if a young person enjoys making art, it may be beneficial to connect them with a local artists collaborative. Or, if a young person is a parent, connecting them with a parenting skills course may help them to improve their relationship with their child as well as connect with other parents. Through connections with these social institutions in their communities, young people can form prosocial support systems while capitalizing on their efforts toward identity projects. The criminal justice system must shift its approach to consider developing prosocial networks as integral to the rehabilitation and desistance processes.

Employment

For emerging adults, it seems that employment in and of itself is not enough of a turning point to facilitate desistance. As demonstrated in the qualitative results, impulsivity and dissatisfaction in the domain of employment resulted in participants quitting their jobs. This is consistent with general emerging adult literature, which highlights that emerging adults are seeking employment they find meaningful and satisfying (Arnett, 2004) and that the exploration of jobs is common and encouraged (Arnett, 2000; Marshall & Butler, 2016). This has important implications for justice-involved emerging adults who already face barriers in accessing employment as a result of their criminal records or lack of work experience.

Practitioners and researchers have traditionally expected that securing a job should function as a sufficient turning point out of crime for young people. Securing work, regardless of satisfaction with employment or the meaning of employment to one's maturation, is expected for young people, especially those engaging in reentry. However, both the quality of employment and its meaningfulness to the transition to adulthood play a role in influencing how successful this turning point is for justice-involved emerging adults. This generational difference in how employment functions for Millennials and Generation Z as a turning point is imperative for criminal justice stakeholders to understand and embrace, including researchers and practitioners. For young people to be successful in their desistance, they need to access opportunities for career exploration and meaning-making that allows them to capitalize on the structures of emerging adulthood to facilitate maturation in line with their peers.

A key conclusion of this text, echoing theories and evidence within the field of emerging adulthood, is that the type, quality, and length of employment should be considered when examining desistance within emerging adulthood. Research on desistance within emerging adulthood should move beyond a dichotomous or economically-based coding of employment (e.g., wages, number of hours worked) in order to reflect the nuances of this domain as a turning point within the life course. Additionally, as criminal justice agents and other professionals work with emerging adults with histories of justice-involvement or engagement in deviant behaviors, they must take care in understanding the differential importance of employment for emerging adults. Justice-involved emerging adults engaging in desistance may be better served by seeking enjoyable and fulfilling employment that fits within the narrative of each emerging adult's future self and long-term career goals.

Practitioners can play an important role in facilitating desistance for emerging adults by supporting their career exploration and development. Consequently, community-based programs, transitional work programs, and probation/parole officers must shift their focus toward understanding the needs of the emerging adults they serve. This includes a focus on the type and quality of employment within the context of each emerging adult's goals. Criminal justice stakeholders supporting young adults' desistance and rehabilitation need to adapt to fit these needs in order to allow for the best outcomes for these individuals as well as for the benefit of their communities.

Given the context of the sample of participants in this study, it is important to highlight the potential impact of community-based interventions that offer a unique framework for delivering interventions targeted at justice-involved emerging adults. Certainly, research has recognized that community-based interventions can fill gaps in the justice system for serving the needs of emerging adults (e.g., Salvatore & Taniguchi, 2012; Schiraldi et al., 2015). This may be especially important in the context of employment, where community-based interventions can serve as a social institution to provide structure and capacity for job exploration.

Civic Engagement

As young people work to find their place in society, civic or community engagement provides another avenue for role exploration. Traditionally in criminology, civic engagement has been a staple of theory for preventing deviance or promoting desistance. Through contributing to society, young people are able to shift their attitudes toward deviance and social institutions (e.g., the police, the law). This allows young people to adhere to social norms, avoid deviance, and in some cases embrace redemption narratives of desistance.

For emerging adults, civic engagement has shifted in line with employment in terms of its role in social maturation. Emerging adulthood represents a time where young people want to explore what civic engagement means to them and the ways in which they can do it for their communities. However, just as with employment, involvement in the justice system such as incarceration or having a criminal record may limit how young people can engage with their communities. For example, young people with criminal records may be restricted from voting or volunteering in their communities. This constrains how they can make contributions to their communities and may curb their investment in trying to make these contributions as a part of their maturation and desistance processes.

Given this, practitioners and policy makers must create opportunities for young people to purposefully get involved in their communities. This includes opportunities for engagement in canvassing and restoring voting rights for people with criminal records. A key implication here may also be in building the opportunities where those entangled in the justice system can work or volunteer to contribute in ways that benefit their communities. This offers an opportunity for cities and local municipalities to hire or engage justice-involved young people in contributing to building better communities through activities that are routine for them and often capitalize on volunteer work, such as maintaining greenery and parks, caring for local gardens, and building housing.

This also offers an opportunity for the justice system to engage local organizations that utilize volunteer or paid work to accomplish their goals, capitalizing on the need of justice-involved emerging adults to connect with social institutions. For example, they can make and sell art for the benefit of local foundations, make care packages for people who struggle with finding secure housing in their communities, make blankets and cold-weather clothing to donate to local charities, or make stuffed animals or other toys for donation to local children's hospitals or charities.

One example that worked well for this sample was involvement in politics, including voting and poll working, attending community meetings, and canvassing/lobbying for criminal justice reform. Connecting young people in the process of reentry with resources and community-based organizations may be central to helping them build attachment to their communities in a prosocial fashion. This, in turn, expands their prosocial support networks and can shift their attitudes toward their communities, providing justice-involved emerging adults with a path toward desistance under this domain of maturation.

Concluding Remarks

The results of this research provide a foundation through which criminal justice agencies, community-based organizations, and policy makers can continue to address the unique needs of justice-involved emerging adults. Emerging adulthood has been recognized as an important population within the context of the life course and developmental criminology. Specialized services for emerging adults have begun to gain attention among policy makers and practitioners. In particular, young adult courts, specialized jail units, diversion programming, and community-based interventions can help serve the unique needs of this population.

As I discussed at the beginning of this conclusion chapter, my perspective toward these conclusions is directed at the criminal justice system and its adaptation to the needs of emerging adults. Just like their peers outside of the justice system, justice-involved emerging adults both deserve and are better served by the opportunity to explore the possibilities of "who they are" and their roles in society. This requires the criminal justice system and its stakeholders to modify their approaches toward practice and punishment to fit the needs of this life stage to support desistance. To do this, the criminal justice system must work to support young people in building identity projects that can provide young people with an "off ramp" from the criminal justice system.

Importantly, not all identities can work for all youth across various contexts as turning points for maturation and desistance. This means that our justice system must be flexible with the young people entangled in it who are working on desistance. These young people need both options and assistance in accessing the resources necessary for their identity projects. This has to be balanced with affording young people the autonomy and agency to explore identity projects, including failing or quitting those that they do not find meaningful. Fundamentally, this proposes a shift in how the justice system handles its clients – and one which is necessary for supporting the desistance of young people under our everchanging social context.

Notes

1 Chicago/North Lawndale Restorative Justice Community Court: https://www.cookcountycourt.org/ABOUT-THE-COURT/Restorative-Justice-Community-Courts
2 San Francisco Young Adult Court: https://sf.courts.ca.gov/divisions/collaborative-courts/young-adult-court
3 Brooklyn Young Adult Court: https://www.innovatingjustice.org/programs/brooklyn-young-adult-court
4 The TRUE unit, Cheshire Correctional Institute: https://www.themarshallproject.org/2018/05/08/the-connecticut-experiment
5 The PACT unit, Middlesex Jail: https://www.middlesexsheriff.org/press-releases/news/young-offender-unit-opens-middlesex-jail-house-correction
6 Transitional Age Youth (TAY) Specialized Probation, San Francisco: https://sf.gov/information/community-supervision-and-specialized-service-division
7 CHOICE intensive probation supervision program, Roxbury Division of the Boston Municipal Court: https://www.mass.gov/info-details/learn-about-probation-programs#:~:text=non%2DCLTL%20participants.-,CHOICE,as%20an%20alternative%20to%20incarceration
8 Lone Star Justice Alliance's Transformative Justice Initiative: https://www.lonestarjusticealliance.org/transformative-justice/
9 Young Adult Diversion Court: https://yadckalamazoo.weebly.com/about-yadc.html
10 CUNY Fatherhood academy: https://www.cuny.edu/academics/academic-programs/model-programs/cuny-fatherhood-academy/
11 ROCA Massachusetts: https://rocainc.org/who-we-work-with/locations/roca-massachusetts-locations/
12 ROCA Baltimore: https://rocainc.org/who-we-work-with/locations/roca-baltimore-location/
13 UTEC: https://utecinc.org/our-programs/
14 State of Connecticut Senate Bill No. 972 https://www.cga.ct.gov/2021/act/Pa/pdf/2021PA-00054-R00SB-00972-PA.PDF
15 State of California Senate Bill No. 1008 https://leginfo.legislature.ca.gov/faces/billTextClient.xhtml?bill_id=202120220SB1008

BIBLIOGRAPHY

Abeling-Judge, D. (2021). Social bonding experiences facilitating desistance in adolescence. *Crime & Delinquency*, *67*(2), 287–315.

Abrams, L. S., & Terry, D. (2017). *Everyday desistance: The transition to adulthood among formerly incarcerated youth*. Rutgers University Press.

Adams, G. R., & Marshall, S. K. (1996). A developmental social psychology of identity: Understanding the person-in-context. *Journal of Adolescence*, *19*(5), 429–442.

Adler, J. M., Dunlop, W. L., Fivush, R., Lilgendahl, J. P., Lodi-Smith, J., McAdams, D. P., McLean, K. C., Pasupathi, M. & Syed, M. (2017). Research methods for studying narrative identity: A primer. *Social Psychological and Personality Science*, *8*(5), 519–527.

Allan, G. (2008). Flexibility, friendship, and family. *Personal Relationships*, *15*(1), 1–16.

Alwin, D. F., Felmlee, D. H., & Kreager, D. A. (2018). Together through time – Social networks and the life course. In D. F. Alwin, D. H. Felmlee, & D. A. Kreager (Eds.), *Social networks and the life course: Integrating the development of human lives and social relational networks* (pp. 479–486). Springer International Publishing.

American Psychological Association. (2015). *APA Dictionary of Psychology* (2nd ed.). https://dictionary.apa.org/

Aquilino, W. S. (2006). Family relationships and support systems in emerging adulthood. In J. J. Arnett & J. L. Tanner (Eds.), *Emerging adults in America: Coming of age in the 21st century* (pp. 193–217). American Psychological Association. https://doi.org/10.1037/11381-008

Arnett, J. J. (1997). Young people's conceptions of the transition to adulthood. *Youth & Society*, *29*(1), 3–23.

Arnett, J. J. (1998). Learning to stand alone: The contemporary American transition to adulthood in cultural and historical context. *Human Development*, *41*(5–6), 295–315.

Arnett, J. J. (2000). Emerging adulthood: A theory of development from the late teens through the twenties. *American Psychologist*, *55*(5), 469.

Arnett, J. J. (2001). Conceptions of the transition to adulthood: Perspectives from adolescence through midlife. *Journal of Adult Development*, *8*(2), 133–143.

Arnett, J. J. (2004). *Emerging adulthood: The winding road from the late teens through the twenties*. Oxford University Press.

Arnett, J. J. (2005). The developmental context of substance use in emerging adulthood. *Journal of Drug Issues*, *35*(2), 235–254.

Arnett, J. J. (2006). Emerging adulthood: Understanding the new way of coming of age. In J. J. Arnett & J. L. Tanner (Eds.), *Emerging adults in America: Coming of age in the 21st century* (pp. 3–19). American Psychological Association.

Arnett, J. J. (2007). Emerging adulthood: What is it, and what is it good for? *Child Development Perspectives*, *1*(2), 68–73.

Arnett, J. J. (2015). The cultural psychology of emerging adulthood. In L. A. Jensen (Ed.), *The Oxford handbook of human development and culture* (pp. 487–501). Oxford University Press.

Arnett, J. J. (2016). Introduction: Emerging adulthood theory and research: Where are we and where should we go. In J. J. Arnett (Ed.) *The Oxford handbook of emerging adulthood* (pp. 1–7). Oxford University Press.

Arnett, J. J., & Jensen, L. A. (2002). A congregation of one: Individualized religious beliefs among emerging adults. *Journal of Adolescent Research*, *17*(5), 451–467.

Arnett, J. J., & Tanner, J. L. (2011). Themes and variations in emerging adulthood across social classes. In J. J. Arnett, M. Kloep, L. B. Hendry, & J. L. Tanner (Eds.) *Debating emerging adulthood: Stage or process*, Oxford University Press.

Arnett, J. J., Žukauskienė, R., & Sugimura, K. (2014). The new life stage of emerging adulthood at ages 18–29 years: Implications for mental health. *The Lancet Psychiatry*, *1*(7), 569–576.

Augustyn, M. B., & Loughran, T. A. (2017). Juvenile waiver as a mechanism of social stratification: A focus on human capital. *Criminology*, *55*(2), 405–437.

Augustyn, M. B., & McGloin, J. M. (2018). Revisiting juvenile waiver: Integrating the incapacitation experience. *Criminology*, *56*(1), 154–190.

Bachman, J. G., O'Malley, P. M., Schulenberg, J. E., Johnston, L. D., Bryant, A. L., & Merline, A. C. (2014). *The decline of substance use in young adulthood: Changes in social activities, roles, and beliefs*. Psychology Press.

Bachman, J. G., & Schulenberg, J. (1993). How part-time work intensity relates to drug use, problem behavior, time use, and satisfaction among high school seniors: Are these consequences or merely correlates? *Developmental Psychology*, *29*(2), 220.

Balsano, A. B. (2005). Youth civic engagement in the United States: Understanding and addressing the impact of social impediments on positive youth and community development. *Applied Developmental Science*, *9*(4), 188–201.

Bamberg, M. (2011). Who am I? Narration and its contribution to self and identity. *Theory & Psychology*, *21*(1), 3–24.

Barnes, J. C., & Beaver, K. M. (2010). An empirical examination of adolescence-limited offending: A direct test of Moffitt's maturity gap thesis. *Journal of Criminal Justice*, *38*(6), 1176–1185.

Barry, C. M., Madsen, S. D., & DeGrace, A. (2016). Growing up with a little help from their friends in emerging adulthood. In J. J. Arnett (Ed.), *The Oxford handbook of emerging adulthood* (pp. 215–229). Oxford University Press.

Berlin, G., Furstenberg, F. F. Jr, & Waters, M. C. (2010). Introducing the issue. *The Future of Children*, *20*(1), 3–18.

Bersani, B. E., & Doherty, E. E. (2018). Desistance from offending in the twenty-first century. *Annual Review of Criminology*, *1*, 311–334.

Bersani, B. E., Laub, J. H., & Nieuwbeerta, P. (2009). Marriage and desistance from crime in the Netherlands: Do gender and socio-historical context matter? *Journal of Quantitative Criminology*, *25*, 3–24.

Bobkowski, P., & Smith, J. (2013). Social media divide: Characteristics of emerging adults who do not use social network websites. *Media, Culture & Society*, *35*(6), 771–781.

Boonstoppel, S. (2019). "It's not about me no more": Fatherhood and mechanisms of desistance among at-risk men. *Journal of Developmental and Life-Course Criminology*, *5*, 335–365.

Bottoms, A., & Shapland, J. (2011). Steps towards desistance among male young adult recidivists. In S. Farrall, M. Hough, S. Maruna, & R. Sparks (Eds.) *Escape routes: Contemporary perspectives on life after punishment* (pp. 43–80). Routledge.

Bouffard, L. A. (2005). The military as a bridging environment in criminal careers: Differential outcomes of the military experience. *Armed Forces & Society*, *31*(2), 273–295.

Braun, V., & Clarke, V. (2006). Using thematic analysis in psychology. *Qualitative Research in Psychology*, *3*(2), 77–101.

Bruner, J. S. (1990). *Acts of meaning*. Harvard University Press.

Burke, P. J., & Reitzes, D. C. (1981). The link between identity and role performance. *Social Psychology Quarterly*, *44*(2), 83–92.

Burke, P. J., & Stets, J. E. (2009). *Identity theory*. Oxford University Press.

Bushway, S. D., Thornberry, T. P., & Krohn, M. D. (2003). Desistance as a developmental process: A comparison of static and dynamic approaches. *Journal of Quantitative Criminology*, *19*(2), 129–153.

Carlson, C. L. (2014). Seeking self-sufficiency: Why emerging adult college students receive and implement parental advice. *Emerging Adulthood*, *2*(4), 257–269.

Carstensen, L. L., Isaacowitz, D. M., & Charles, S. T. (1999). Taking time seriously: A theory of socioemotional selectivity. *American Psychologist*, *54*(3), 165.

Caspi, A., & Moffitt, T. E. (1993). When do individual differences matter? A paradoxical theory of personality coherence. *Psychological Inquiry*, *4*(4), 247–271.

Cauffman, E., & Steinberg, L. (2000). (Im) maturity of judgment in adolescence: Why adolescents may be less culpable than adults. *Behavioral Sciences & the Law*, *18*(6), 741–760.

Charmaz, K. (2006). *Constructing grounded theory: A practical guide through qualitative research*. Sage Publications.

Chassin, L., Pitts, S. C., & Prost, J. (2002). Binge drinking trajectories from adolescence to emerging adulthood in a high-risk sample: Predictors and substance abuse outcomes. *Journal of Consulting and Clinical Psychology*, *70*(1), 67.

Clausen, J. A. (1986). *The life course – A sociological perspective*. Prentice-Hall.

Conrad, C., Neumann, A., Haworth, J. G., & Scott, P. (1993). *Qualitative research in higher education: Experiencing alternative perspective and approaches*. Ginn Press.

Copp, J. E., Giordano, P. C., Longmore, M. A., & Manning, W. D. (2019). The development of attitudes toward intimate partner violence: An examination of key correlates among a sample of young adults. *Journal of Interpersonal Violence*, *34*(7), 1357–1387.

Côté, J. E. (2000). *Arrested adulthood: The changing nature of maturity and identity*. New York University Press.

Côté, J. E. (2002). The role of identity capital in the transition to adulthood: The individualization thesis examined. *Journal of Youth Studies*, *5*(2), 117–134.

Côté, J. E. (2006). Emerging adulthood as an institutionalized moratorium: Risks and benefits to identity formation. In J. J. Arnett & J. L. Tanner (Eds.), *Emerging adults in America: Coming of age in the 21st century* (pp. 85–116). American Psychological Association. https://doi.org/10.1037/11381-004

Côté, J. E. (2014). The dangerous myth of emerging adulthood: An evidence-based critique of a flawed developmental theory. *Applied Developmental Science*, *18*(4), 177–188.

Côté, J. E. (2015). Identity formation research from a critical perspective: Is a social science developing? In McLean, K. C., & Syed, M. (Eds.), *The oxford handbook of identity development* (pp. 527–538). Oxford University Press.

Côté, J. E., & Allahar, A. L. (2006). *Critical youth studies: A Canadian focus*. Pearson Education.

Côté, J. E., & Bynner, J. M. (2008). Changes in the transition to adulthood in the UK and Canada: The role of structure and agency in emerging adulthood. *Journal of Youth Studies*, *11*(3), 251–268.

Côté, J. E., & Levine, C. G. (2002). *Identity, formation, agency, and culture: A social psychological synthesis*. Erlbaum.

Coyle, B. (2019). 'What the f** k is maturity?': Young adulthood, subjective maturity and desistance from crime. *The British Journal of Criminology*, *59*(5), 1178–1198.

Craig, J., & Foster, H. (2013). Desistance in the transition to adulthood: The roles of marriage, military, and gender. *Deviant Behavior*, *34*(3), 208–223.

Creswell, J. W. (2007). *Qualitative inquiry and research design: Choosing among five approaches*. Sage Publications Inc.

Davis, M., Banks, S., Fisher, W., & Grudzinskas, A. (2004). Longitudinal patterns of offending during the transition to adulthood in youth from the mental health system. *The Journal of Behavioral Health Services & Research*, *31*(4), 351–366.

DeLuca, S., Clampet-Lundquist, S., & Edin, K. (2016). *Coming of age in the other America*. Russell Sage Foundation.

Demir, M., & Özdemir, M. (2010). Friendship, Need satisfaction and happiness. *Journal of Happiness Studies*, *11*, 243–259.

Deterding, N. M., & Waters, M. C. (2018). Flexible coding of in-depth interviews: A twenty-first-century approach. *Sociological Methods & Research*, 50(2), 708–739.

Dietrich, J., & Salmela-Aro, K. (2016). Emerging adults and work: A model of phase-adequate engagement. In J. J. Arnett (Ed.), *The Oxford handbook of emerging adulthood* (pp. 334–345). Oxford University Press.

Dmitrieva, J., Monahan, K. C., Cauffman, E., & Steinberg, L. (2012). Arrested development: The effects of incarceration on the development of psychosocial maturity. *Development and Psychopathology*, *24*(3), 1073–1090.

Doherty, E. E., & Ensminger, M. E. (2014). Do the adult criminal careers of African Americans fit the "facts"? *Journal of Criminal Justice*, *42*(6), 517–526.

Droppelmann, C. (2021). *Transitions out of crime: New approaches on desistance in late adolescence*. Routledge.

Dubas, J. S., & Petersen, A. C. (1996). Geographical distance from parents and adjustment during adolescence and young adulthood. *New Directions for Child and Adolescent Development*, *1996*(71), 3–19.

Duwe, G. (2015). An outcome evaluation of a prison work release program: Estimating its effects on recidivism, employment, and cost avoidance. *Criminal Justice Policy Review*, *26*(6), 531–554.

Elder, G. H. (1986). Military times and turning points in men's lives. *Developmental Psychology*, *22*(2), 233–245.

Elder, G. H. (1998). The life course as developmental theory. *Child Development*, *69*, 1–12.

Emirbayer, M., & Mische, A. (1998). What is agency? *American Journal of Sociology*, *103*(4), 962–1023.

Erikson, E. H. (1950). *Childhood and society*. Norton.

Erikson, E. H. (1963). *Childhood and society* (2nd ed.). Norton.

Erikson, E. H. (1968). *Identity: Youth and crisis*. W. W. Norton & Company.

Erikson, E. H. (1970). Autobiographic notes on the identity crisis. *Daedalus*, *99* (4), 730–759.

Evans, K., & Heinz, W. R. (1994). *Becoming adults in England and Germany*. Anglo-German Foundation.

Fader, J. J. (2013). *Falling back: Incarceration and transitions to adulthood among urban youth*. Rutgers University Press.

Fagan, J. (1989). Cessation of family violence: Deterrence and dissuasion. *Crime and Justice*, *11*, 377–425.

Farrall, S. (2002). *Rethinking what works with offenders*. Willan Publishing.

Farrall, S., & Bowling, B. (1999). Structuration, human development and desistance from crime. *British Journal of Criminology*, *39*(2), 253–268.

Farrall, S., & Calverley, A. (2006). *Understanding desistance from crime: Theoretical directions in resettlement and rehabilitation*. Open University Press.

Farrall, S., Sharpe, G., Hunter, B., & Calverley, A. (2011). Theorizing structural and individual-level processes in desistance and persistence: Outlining an integrated perspective. *Australian & New Zealand Journal of Criminology*, *44*(2), 218–234.

Farrington, D. P., & West, D. J. (1995). Effects of marriage, separation, and children on offending by adult males. *Current Perspectives on Aging and the Life Cycle*, 4, 249–281.

Feiring, C. (1996). Concepts of romance in 15-year-old adolescents. *Journal of Research on Adolescence*, 6(2), 181–200.

Fingerman, K. L., Cheng, Y. P., Tighe, L., Birditt, K. S., & Zarit, S. (2011). Relationships between young adults and their parents. In A. Booth, S. L. Brown, N. S. Landale, W. D. Manning, & S. M. McHale (Eds). *Early adulthood in a family context* (pp. 59–85). Springer New York.

Fingerman, K. L., & Yahirun, J. J. (2016). Emerging adulthood in the context of family. In J. J. Arnett (Ed.), *The Oxford handbook of emerging adulthood* (pp. 163–176). Oxford University Press.

Flanagan, C., & Levine, P. (2010). Civic engagement and the transition to adulthood. *The Future of Children*, *20*(1), 159–179.

Forrest, W. (2014). Cohabitation, relationship quality, and desistance from crime. *Journal of Marriage and Family*, *76*(3), 539–556.

Fox, K. J. (2015). Theorizing community integration as desistance-promotion. *Criminal Justice and Behavior*, *42*(1), 82–94.

Fox, K. J. (2016). Civic commitment: Promoting desistance through community integration. *Punishment & Society*, *18*(1), 68–94.

Fox, J., & Warber, K. M. (2013). Romantic relationship development in the age of Facebook: An exploratory study of emerging adults' perceptions, motives, and behaviors. *Cyberpsychology, Behavior, and Social Networking*, *16*(1), 3–7.
Frisen, A., & Wängqvist, M. (2011). Emerging adults in Sweden: Identity formation in the light of love, work, and family. *Journal of Adolescent Research*, *26*(2), 200–221.
Furstenberg, F. F. (2006). Diverging development: The not-so-invisible hand of social class in the United States. In B. J. Risman (Ed.), Families as they really are (pp. 276–294). W.W. Norton & Company.
Furstenberg, F. F. (2008). The intersections of social class and the transition to adulthood. *New Directions for Child and Adolescent Development*, *2008*(119), 1–10. https://doi.org/10.1002/cd.205
Furstenberg, F. F. Jr. (2010). On a new schedule: Transitions to adulthood and family change. *The Future of Children*, *20*(1), 67–87.
Furstenberg, F. F., Rumbaut, R. G., & Settersten, R. A. (2005). On the frontier of adulthood: Emerging themes and new directions. In R. A. Settersten, Jr., F. F. Furstenberg, & R. G. Rumbaut (Eds.), *On the frontier of adulthood: Theory, research, and public policy* (pp. 3–25). University of Chicago Press.
Galambos, N. L., & Costigan, C. L. (2003). Emotional and personality development in adolescence. In R. M. Lerner, M. A. Easterbrooks, & J. Mistry (Eds.), *Handbook of psychology: Developmental psychology* (Vol. 6, pp. 351–372). John Wiley & Sons, Inc.
Galambos, N. L., Turner, P. K., & Tilton-Weaver, L. C. (2005). Chronological and subjective age in emerging adulthood: The crossover effect. *Journal of Adolescent Research*, *20*(5), 538–556.
Gibbs, G.R. (2007). *Analyzing qualitative data*. Sage Publications.
Giordano, P. C., Cernkovich, S. A., & Rudolph, J. L. (2002). Gender, crime, and desistance: Toward a theory of cognitive transformation. *American Journal of Sociology*, *107*(4), 990–1064.
Giordano, P. C., Schroeder, R. D., & Cernkovich, S. A. (2007). Emotions and crime over the life course: A neo-Meadian perspective on criminal continuity and change. *American Journal of Sociology*, *112*(6), 1603–1661.
Glaser, B., & Strauss, A. (1967). *The discovery of grounded theory: Strategies for qualitative research*. Aldine.
Glaser, B. G. (1965). The constant comparative method of qualitative analysis. *Social Problems*, *12*(4), 436–445.
Glueck, S., & Glueck, E. (1937). *Later criminal careers*. The Commonwealth Fund.
Glueck, S., & Glueck, E. (1940). *Juvenile delinquents grown up*. The Commonwealth Fund.
Glueck, S., & Glueck, E. (1943). *Criminal careers in retrospect*. The Commonwealth Fund.
Glueck, S., & Glueck, E. (1968). *Delinquents and nondelinquents in perspective*. Harvard University Press.
Glueck, S., & Glueck, E. T. (1974). *Of delinquency and crime: A panorama of years of search and research*. CC Thomas.
Goldie, P. (2003). One's remembered past: Narrative thinking, emotion, and the external perspective. *Philosophical Papers*, *32*(3), 301–319.
Gottfredson, M. R., & Hirschi, T. (1990). *A general theory of crime*. Stanford University Press.

Greenberg, D. F. (1977). Crime deterrence research and social policy. *Policy Studies Review Annual*, *1*, 461.

Greenberger, E., Josselson, R., Knerr, C., & Knerr, B. (1975). The measurement and structure of psychosocial maturity. *Journal of Youth and Adolescence*, *4*(2), 127–143.

Greenberger, E., & Sørensen, A. B. (1974). Toward a concept of psychosocial maturity. *Journal of Youth and Adolescence*, *3*(4), 329–358.

Greenberger, E., & Steinberg, L. (1986). *When teenagers work: The psychological and social costs of adolescent employment*. Basic Books.

Greene, A. L., Wheatley, S. M., & Aldava, J. F. IV (1992). Stages on life's way: Adolescents' implicit theories of the life course. *Journal of Adolescent Research*, *7*(3), 364–381.

Guan, S. S. A., & Fuligni, A. J. (2016). Changes in parent, sibling, and peer support during the transition to young adulthood. *Journal of Research on Adolescence*, *26*(2), 286–299.

Habermas, T., & Bluck, S. (2000). Getting a life: The emergence of the life story in adolescence. *Psychological Bulletin*, *126*(5), 748.

Habermas, T., & Köber, C. (2015). Autobiographical reasoning is constitutive for narrative identity: The role of the life story for personal continuity. In K. C. McLean & M. Syed (Eds.) *The Oxford handbook of identity development* (pp. 149–165). Oxford University Press.

Hagestad, G. O., & Settersten, R. A. Jr (2017). Aging: It's interpersonal! Reflections from two life course migrants. *The Gerontologist*, *57*(1), 136–144.

Halsey, M., & Deegan, S. (2015). *Young offenders: Crime, prison and struggles for desistance*. Springer.

Harding, D. J., & Harris, H. M. (2020). *After prison: Navigating adulthood in the shadow of the justice system*. Russell Sage Foundation.

Haynie, D. L. (2001). Delinquent peers revisited: Does network structure matter? *American Journal of Sociology*, *106*(4), 1013–1057.

Healy, D. (2013). Changing fate? Agency and the desistance process. *Theoretical Criminology*, *17*(4), 557–574.

Hill, J. M., Blokland, A. A., & van der Geest, V. R. (2016). Desisting from crime in emerging adulthood: Adult roles and the maturity gap. *Journal of Research in Crime and Delinquency*, *53*(4), 506–535.

Hirschi, T. (1969). *Causes of delinquency*. University of California Press.

Hirschi, T., & Gottfredson, M. (1983). Age and the explanation of crime. *American Journal of Sociology*, *89*(3), 552–584.

Hoge, R., Johnson, B., & Luidens, D. A. (1993). Determinants of church involvement of young adults who grew up in Presbyterian churches. *Journal for the Scientific Study of Religion*, *32*(3), 242–255.

Horney, J., Osgood, D. W., & Marshall, I. H. (1995). Criminal careers in the short-term: Intra-individual variability in crime and its relation to local life circumstances. *American Sociological Review*, *60*, 655–673.

Jang, S. J., & Rhodes, J. R. (2012). General strain and non-strain theories: A study of crime in emerging adulthood. *Journal of Criminal Justice*, *40*(3), 176–186.

Jian, L., Pettus-Davis, C., & Kohl, P. L. (2022). Young fathers in jail: Associations between father experiences, father–child relationships, and community stability. *Victims & Offenders*, *17*(4), 571–596.

Johnson, W. L., Giordano, P. C., Manning, W. D., & Longmore, M. A. (2011). Parent–child relations and offending during young adulthood. *Journal of Youth and Adolescence*, *40*, 786–799.

Johnston, L. D., O'Malley, P. M., Bachman, J. G., & Schulenberg, J. E. (2010). Monitoring the Future: National Survey Results on Drug Use, 1975–2009. Volume I: Secondary School Students. NIH Publication No. 10-7584. *National Institute on Drug Abuse (NIDA)*. https://books.google.com/books?hl=en&lr=&id=TQMRXa4Ja7MC&oi=fnd&pg=PP1&dq=Johnston,+L.+D.,++O%E2%80%99Malley,+P.+M.,+Bachman,+J.+G.,+%26+Schulenberg,+J.+E.+(2010).+Monitoring+the+Future:+National+Survey+Results+on+Drug+Use,+1975%E2%80%932009.+Volume+I:+Secondary+School+Students.+NIH+Publication+No.+10-7584.+National+Institute+on+Drug+Abuse+(NIDA).&ots=9ZsOhvvPdJ&sig=CpuZ5T8FXPUX2eVNU4dl8_Sytbg#v=onepage&q&f=false

Kazemian, L. (2007). Desistance from crime: Theoretical, empirical, methodological, and policy considerations. *Journal of Contemporary Criminal Justice*, *23*(1), 5–27.

Keniston, K. (1971). Psychological development and historical change. *The Journal of Interdisciplinary History*, *2*(2), 329–345.

Kiecolt, K. J. (1994). Stress and the decision to change oneself: A theoretical model. *Social Psychology Quarterly*, *57*(1), 49–63.

King, S. (2013). Transformative agency and desistance from crime. *Criminology and Criminal Justice*, *13*, 317–335.

King, P. M., & Kitchener, K. S. (2016). Cognitive development in the emerging adult: The emergence of complex cognitive skills. In J. J. Arnett (Ed.), *The Oxford handbook of emerging adulthood* (pp. 105–125). Oxford University Press.

King, R. D., Massoglia, M., & MacMillan, R. (2007). The context of marriage and crime: Gender, the propensity to marry, and offending in early adulthood. *Criminology*, *45*(1), 33–65.

Klimstra, T. A., Hale, W. W. III, Raaijmakers, Q. A., Branje, S. J., & Meeus, W. H. (2010). Identity formation in adolescence: Change or stability? *Journal of Youth and Adolescence*, *39*(2), 150–162.

Kohli, M. (1988). Ageing as a challenge for sociological theory. *Ageing and Society*, *8*, 367–394.

Kohli, M. (2007). The institutionalization of the life course: Looking back to look ahead. *Research in Human Development*, *4*, 253–271.

Kolb, S. M. (2012). Grounded theory and the constant comparative method: Valid research strategies for educators. *Journal of Emerging Trends in Educational Research and Policy Studies*, *3*(1), 83–86.

Kreager, D. A., Felmlee, D. H., & Alwin, D. F. (2018). Strategies for integrating network and life course perspectives. In D. F. Alwin, D. H. Felmlee, & D. A. Kreager (Eds.), *Social networks and the life course: Integrating the development of human lives and social relational networks* (pp. 479–486). Springer International Publishing.

Kroger, J., & Marcia, J. E. (2011). The identity statuses: Origins, meanings, and interpretations. In S. J. Schwartz, K. Luyckx, & V. L. Vignoles (Eds.), *Handbook of identity theory and research* (pp. 31–53). Springer.

Kroger, J., Martinussen, M., & Marcia, J. E. (2010). Identity status change during adolescence and young adulthood: A meta-analysis. *Journal of Adolescence*, *33*(5), 683–698.

Labouvie, E. (1996). Maturing out of substance use: Selection and self-correction. *Journal of Drug Issues*, *26*(2), 457–476.

Laub, J., Nagin, D., & Samson, R. (1998). Trajectories of change in criminal offending: Good marriages and the desistance process. *American Sociological Review*, *63*, 225–238.

Laub, J. H., Rowan, Z. R., & Sampson, R. J. (2018). The age-graded theory of informal social control. In D. P. Farrington, L. Kazemian, & A. R. Piquero (Eds.) *The Oxford handbook of developmental and life-course criminology* (pp. 295–322). Oxford University Press.

Laub, J. H., & Sampson, R. J. (1991). The Sutherland-Glueck debate: On the sociology of criminological knowledge. *American Journal of Sociology*, *96*(6), 1402–1440.

Laub, J. H., & Sampson, R. J. (2001). Understanding desistance from crime. *Crime and Justice*, *28*, 1–69.

Laub, J. H., & Sampson, R. J. (2003). *Shared beginnings, divergent lives: Delinquent boys to age 70*. Harvard University Press.

Laub, J. H., & Sampson, R. J. (2020). life-course and developmental criminology: Looking back, moving forward—ASC division of developmental and life-course criminology inaugural David P. Farrington lecture, 2017. *Journal of Developmental and Life-Course Criminology*, *6*, 158–171.

Lee, J. S., & Waithaka, E. N. (2017). The intersections of marginalized social identities in the transition to adulthood: A demographic profile. *Emerging Adulthood*, *5*(3), 151–163.

Levinson, D. J. (1986). A conception of adult development. *American Psychologist*, *41*(1), 3.

Liang, B., Spencer, R., Brogan, D., & Corral, M. (2008). Mentoring relationships from early adolescence through emerging adulthood: A qualitative analysis. *Journal of Vocational Behavior*, *72*(2), 168–182.

Lindsay, S. L. (2022). Damned if you do, damned if you don't: How formerly incarcerated men navigate the labor market with prison credentials. *Criminology*, *60*(3), 455–479.

Lloyd, K. M., & Turanovic, J. J. (2020). Instrumental support from parents and substance use during the transition to adulthood. *Journal of Developmental and Life-Course Criminology*, *6*, 477–498.

Lopez, J., & Scott, J. (2000). *Social structure*. Open University Press.

Loughran, T. A., Mulvey, E. P., Schubert, C. A., Fagan, J., Piquero, A. R., & Losoya, S. H. (2009). Estimating a dose-response relationship between length of stay and future recidivism in serious juvenile offenders. *Criminology*, *47*(3), 699–740.

Luyckx, K., Goossens, L., Soenens, B., & Beyers, W. (2006). Unpacking commitment and exploration: Preliminary validation of an integrative model of late adolescent identity formation. *Journal of Adolescence*, *29*(3), 361–378.

Magolda, M. B., & Taylor, K. (2016). Developing self-authorship in college to navigate emerging adulthood. In J. J. Arnett (Ed.), *The Oxford handbook of emerging adulthood* (pp. 299–315). Oxford University Press.

Manza, J., & Uggen, C. (2004). Punishment and democracy: Disenfranchisement of nonincarcerated felons in the United States. *Perspectives on Politics*, *2*(3), 491–505.

Manza, J., & Uggen, C. (2008). *Locked out: Felon disenfranchisement and American democracy*. Oxford University Press.

Marcia, J. E. (1966). Development and validation of ego-identity status. *Journal of Personality and Social Psychology*, *3*(5), 551.

Marcia, J. E. (1980). Identity in adolescence. *Handbook of Adolescent Psychology*, *9*(11), 159–187.

Marcus, R. F. (2009). Cross-sectional study of violence in emerging adulthood. *Aggressive Behavior: Official Journal of the International Society for Research on Aggression*, *35*(2), 188–202.

Marsden, P. V. (2018). Life course events and network composition. In D. F. Alwin, D. H. Felmlee, & D. A. Kreager (Eds.), *Social networks and the life course: Integrating the development of human lives and social relational networks* (pp. 89–113). Springer International Publishing.

Marshall, E. A., & Butler, K. (2016). School-to-work transitions in emerging adulthood. In J. J. Arnett (Ed.), *The Oxford handbook of emerging adulthood* (pp. 316–333). Oxford University Press.

Maruna, S. (2001). *Making good: How ex-convicts reform and rebuild their lives.* American Psychological Association.

Maruna, S., & Copes, H. (2005). What have we learned from five decades of neutralization research? *Crime and Justice*, *32*, 221–320.

Maruna, S., & Roy, K. (2007). Amputation or reconstruction? Notes on the concept of "knifing off" and desistance from crime. *Journal of Contemporary Criminal Justice*, *23*(1), 104–124.

Massoglia, M., & Uggen, C. (2010). Settling down and aging out: Toward an interactionist theory of desistance and the transition to adulthood. *American Journal of Sociology*, *116*(2), 543–582.

Matza, D. (1964). *Delinquency and drift.* Wiley.

Mawson, E., Best, D., Beckwith, M., Dingle, G. A., & Lubman, D. I. (2015). Social identity, social networks and recovery capital in emerging adulthood: A pilot study. *Substance Abuse Treatment, Prevention, and Policy*, *10*, 1–11.

Mayseless, O., & Scharf, M. (2003). What does it mean to be an adult? The Israeli experience. *New Directions for Child and Adolescent Development*, *2003*(100), 5–20.

McAdams, D. P. (1988). *Power, intimacy, and the life story: Personological inquiries into identity.* Guilford.

McAdams, D. P. (1993). *The stories we live by: Personal myths and the making of the self.* Morrow.

McAdams, D. P. (1997). The case for unity in the (post) modern self. In R. D. Ashmore & L. Jussim (Eds). *Self and Identity: Fundamental Issues* (pp. 46–78). Oxford University Press. https://books.google.com/books?hl=en&lr=&id=N3BZT1QK7_AC&oi=fnd&pg=PA46&dq=McAdams,+D.+P.+(1997).+The+case+for+unity+in+the+(post)+modern+self.+Self+and+Identity,+46%E2%80%9378.+&ots=j9NuJOAcJe&sig=8Xa6ZT5a0pLKUg0X9lA7hCpovlQ#v=onepage&q&f=false

McAdams, D. P. (2001). The psychology of life stories. *Review of General Psychology*, *5*(2), 100.

McAdams, D. P. (2006a). *The redemptive self: Stories Americans live by.* Oxford University Press

McAdams, D. P. (2006b). The problem of narrative coherence. *Journal of Constructivist Psychology*, *19*(2), 109–125.

McAdams, D. P. (2008). Personal narratives and the life story. In O. P. John, R. W. Robins, & L. A. Pervin (Eds.), *Handbook of personality: Theory and research* (3rd ed., pp. 242–262). Guilford.

McAdams, D. P. (2013). The psychological self as actor, agent, and author. *Perspectives on Psychological Science*, *8*(3), 272–295.

McAdams, D. P., & Cox, K. S. (2010). Self and identity across the life span. In R. M. Lerner, M. E. Lamb, & A. M. Freund (Eds.), *The handbook of life-span development* (pp. 160–207). John Wiley & Sons, Inc.

McAdams, D. P., & de St. Aubin, E. D. (1992). A theory of generativity and its assessment through self-report, behavioral acts, and narrative themes in autobiography. *Journal of Personality and Social Psychology*, *62*(6), 1003.

McAdams, D. P., Hart, H. M., & Maruna, S. (1998). The anatomy of generativity. In D. P. McAdams & E. de St. Aubin (Eds.), *Generativity and adult development: How and why we care for the next generation* (pp. 7–43). American Psychological Association.

McAdams, D. P., Hoffman, B. J., Day, R., & Mansfield, E. D. (1996). Themes of agency and communion in significant autobiographical scenes. *Journal of Personality*, *64*(2), 339–377.

McAdams, D. P., Josselson, R., & Lieblich, A. (2006). *Identity and story: Creating self in narrative*. Washington, DC: American Psychological Association.

McAdams, D. P., & Zapata-Gietl, C. (2015). Three strands of identity development across the human life course: Reading Erik Erikson in full. In K. C. McLean & M. Syed (Eds.), *The Oxford handbook of identity development* (pp. 81–96). Oxford University Press.

McCabe, A., & Dinh, K. T. (2018). High points, low points, turning points: Life stories of Cambodian American youth. *Journal of Southeast Asian American Education and Advancement*, *13*(1), 1–28.

McLean, K. C., & Pratt, M. W. (2006). Life's little (and big) lessons: Identity statuses and meaning-making in the turning point narratives of emerging adults. *Developmental Psychology*, *42*(4), 714.

McLean, K. C., Syed, M., & Shucard, H. (2016a). Bringing identity content to the fore: Links to identity development processes. *Emerging Adulthood*, *4*(5), 356–364.

McLean, K. C., Syed, M., Yoder, A., & Greenhoot, A. F. (2016b). The role of domain content in understanding identity development processes. *Journal of Research on Adolescence*, *26*(1), 60–75.

Mizel, M. L., & Abrams, L. S. (2018). What I'd tell my 16-year-old self: Criminal desistance, young adults, and psychosocial maturation. *International Journal of Offender Therapy and Comparative Criminology*, *62*(10), 3038–3057.

Modecki, K. L. (2008). Addressing gaps in the maturity of judgment literature: Age differences and delinquency. *Law and Human Behavior*, *32*, 78–91.

Moffitt, T. E. (1993). Adolescence-limited and life-course-persistent antisocial behavior: A developmental taxonomy. *Psychological Review*, *100*(4), 674.

Moffitt, T. E., Caspi, A., Harrington, H., & Milne, B. J. (2002). Males on the life-course-persistent and adolescence-limited antisocial pathways: Follow-up at age 26 years. *Development and Psychopathology*, *14*(1), 179–207.

Monahan, K. C., Steinberg, L., Cauffman, E., & Mulvey, E. P. (2009). Trajectories of antisocial behavior and psychosocial maturity from adolescence to young adulthood. *Developmental Psychology*, *45*(6), 1654.

Monahan, K. C., Steinberg, L., Cauffman, E., & Mulvey, E. P. (2013). Psychosocial (im) maturity from adolescence to early adulthood: Distinguishing between adolescence-limited and persisting antisocial behavior. *Development and Psychopathology*, *25*(4pt1), 1093–1105.

Mortimer, J. T., Harley, C., & Aronson, P. J. (1999). How do prior experiences in the workplace set the stage for transitions to adulthood. In A. Booth, A. C. Crouter, & M. J. Shanahan (Eds.), *Transitions to adulthood in a changing economy: No work, no family, no future* (pp. 131–159). Praeger Publishers.

Mortimer, J. T., & Shanahan, M. J. (Eds.). (2007). *Handbook of the life course.* Springer Science & Business Media.

Murdock, G. (1949). *Social structure.* MacMillan.

Nader, E. S. (2019). *Desistance among emerging adults: A mixed methods approach to understanding identity formation, community, and relationships* [Doctoral dissertation]. University of Massachusetts Lowell.

Nader, E. S., & Davies Robinson, A. (2023). Reconceptualizing social bonds for emerging adults. *Criminal Justice and Behavior*, 50(5), 708–728.

Nagin, D. S. (2005). *Group-based modeling of development.* Harvard University Press.

Nagin, D. S., Farrington, D. P., & Moffitt, T. E. (1995). Life-course trajectories of different types of offenders. *Criminology*, *33*(1), 111–139.

Newton, D., Day, A., Giles, M., Wodak, J., Graffam, J., & Baldry, E. (2018). The impact of vocational education and training programs on recidivism: A systematic review of current experimental evidence. *International Journal of Offender Therapy and Comparative Criminology*, *62*(1), 187–207.

Nguyen, H., & Loughran, T. A. (2018). On the measurement and identification of turning points in criminology. *Annual Review of Criminology*, *1*, 335–358.

O'Connor, T. G., Allen, J. P., Bell, K. L., & Hauser, S. T. (1996). Adolescent-parent relationships and leaving home in young adulthood. *New Directions for Child and Adolescent Development*, *1996*(71), 39–52.

Osgood, D. W., Foster, E. M., Flanagan, C., & Ruth, G. R. (2005). *On your own without a net: The transition to adulthood for vulnerable populations.* University of Chicago Press.

Padilla-Walker, L. M. (2016). Moral development during emerging adulthood. In J. J. Arnett (Ed.), *The Oxford handbook of emerging adulthood* (pp. 449–463). Oxford University Press.

Pager, D. (2003). The mark of a criminal record. *American Journal of Sociology*, *108*(5), 937–975.

Pager, D., Western, B., & Sugie, N. (2009). Sequencing disadvantage: Barriers to employment facing young black and white men with criminal records. *The ANNALS of the American Academy of Political and Social Science*, *623*(1), 195–213.

Pasupathi, M., & Mansour, E. (2006). Adult age differences in autobiographical reasoning in narratives. *Developmental Psychology*, *42*(5), 798.

Pasupathi, M., Mansour, E., & Brubaker, J. R. (2007). Developing a life story: Constructing relations between self and experience in autobiographical narratives. *Human Development*, *50*(2–3), 85–110.

Paternoster, R., & Bushway, S. (2009). Desistance and the" feared self": Toward an identity theory of criminal desistance. *The Journal of Criminal Law and Criminology*, *99*(4), 1103–1156.

Patton, M. Q. (2015). *Qualitative research and methods: Integrating theory and practice.* Sage Publications.

Perry, W. G. Jr. (1999). *Forms of intellectual and ethical development in the college years: A scheme.* Jossey-Bass Publishers.

Piaget, J. (1951). *Play, dreams, and imitation in childhood.* Routledge and Kegan Paul Ltd.

Piquero, A. R. (2015). Understanding race/ethnicity differences in offending across the life course: Gaps and opportunities. *Journal of Developmental and Life-Course Criminology, 1*, 21–32.

Piquero, A. R., Brame, R., Mazerolle, P., & Haapanen, R. (2002). Crime in emerging adulthood. *Criminology, 40*(1), 137–170.

Piquero, A. R., & Brezina, T. (2001). Testing Moffitt's account of adolescence-limited delinquency. *Criminology, 39*(2), 353–370.

Porfeli, E. J., Lee, B., Vondracek, F. W., & Weigold, I. K. (2011). A multi-dimensional measure of vocational identity status. *Journal of Adolescence, 34*(5), 853–871.

Presser, L. (2004). Violent offenders, moral selves: Constructing identities and accounts in the research interview. *Social Problems, 51*(1), 82–101.

Presser, L., & Sandberg, S. (Eds.). (2015). *Narrative criminology: Understanding stories of crime.* New York University Press.

Ricoeur, P. (1992). *Oneself as another.* University of Chicago Press.

Rise, J., Sheeran, P., & Hukkelberg, S. (2010). The role of self-identity in the theory of planned behavior: A meta-analysis. *Journal of Applied Social Psychology, 40*(5), 1085–1105.

Rocque, M. (2012). *Understanding the relationship between maturation and desistance from crime: A life-course developmental approach* [Doctoral dissertation]. Northeastern University.

Rocque, M. (2015). The lost concept: The (re) emerging link between maturation and desistance from crime. *Criminology & Criminal Justice, 15*(3), 340–360.

Rocque, M. (2017). *Desistance from crime: New advances in theory and research.* Palgrave Macmillan.

Rocque, M., Beckley, A. L., & Piquero, A. R. (2019). Psychosocial maturation, race, and desistance from crime. *Journal of Youth and Adolescence, 48*, 1403–1417.

Rocque, M., Posick, C., & Paternoster, R. (2016). Identities through time: An exploration of identity change as a cause of desistance. *Justice Quarterly, 33*(1), 45–72.

Rocque, M., Posick, C., & White, H. R. (2015). Growing up is hard to do: An empirical evaluation of maturation and desistance. *Journal of Developmental and Life-Course Criminology, 1*, 350–384.

Roscoe, B., Diana, M. S., & Brooks, R. H. (1987). Early, middle, and late adolescents' views on dating and factors influencing partner selection. *Adolescence, 22*(85), 59.

Rumgay, J. (2004). Scripts for safer survival: Pathways out of female crime. *The Howard Journal of Criminal Justice, 43*(4), 405–419.

Sakala, L., Courtney, L., Matei, A., & Harvell, S. (2020). A guide to community strategies for improving emerging adults' safety and well-being. *Urban Institute.*

Salvatore, C. (2017). The emerging adulthood gap: Integrating emerging adulthood into life course criminology. *International Social Science Review, 93*(1), 2.

Salvatore, C., & Taniguchi, T. A. (2012). Do social bonds matter for emerging adults? *Deviant Behavior, 33*(9), 738–756.

Salvatore, C., Taniguchi, T., & Welsh, W. N. (2012). Is emerging adulthood influencing Moffitt's developmental taxonomy? Adding the "prolonged" adolescent offender. *Western Criminology Review, 13*(1), 1.

Sampson, R. J., & Laub, J. H. (1993). *Crime in the making: Pathways and turning points through life.* Harvard University Press.

Sampson, R. J., & Laub, J. H. (2005). A general age-graded theory of crime: Lessons learned and the future of life-course criminology. In D. Farrington (Ed.), *Advances in criminological theory* (pp. 161–185). Transaction Publishers.

Sampson, R. J., Laub, J. H., & Wimer, C. (2006). Does marriage reduce crime? A counterfactual approach to within-individual causal effects. *Criminology*, *44*(3), 465–508.

Sampson, R. J., Raudenbush, S. W., & Earls, F. (1997). Neighborhoods and violent crime: A multilevel study of collective efficacy. *Science*, *277*(5328), 918–924.

Savolainen, J. (2009). Work, family and criminal desistance: Adult social bonds in a Nordic welfare state. *The British Journal of Criminology*, *49*(3), 285–304.

Scheer, S. D., Unger, D. G., & Brown, M. B. (1996). Adolescents becoming adults: Attributes for adulthood. *Adolescence*, *31*(121), 127.

Schiraldi, V., Western, B., & Bradner, K. (2015). *Community-based responses to justice-involved young adults.* US Department of Justice, Office of Justice Programs, National Institute of Justice.

Schwartz, S. J. (2001). The evolution of Eriksonian and, neo-Eriksonian identity theory and research: A review and integration. *Identity: an International Journal of Theory and Research*, *1*(1), 7–58.

Schwartz, S. J., Côté, J. E., & Arnett, J. J. (2005). Identity and agency in emerging adulthood: Two developmental routes in the individualization process. *Youth & Society*, *37*(2), 201–229.

Schwartz, S. J., Zamboanga, B. L., Luyckx, K., Meca, A., & Richie, R. (2016). Identity development in emerging adulthood. In J. J. Arnett (Ed.), *The Oxford handbook of emerging adulthood* (pp. 401–420). Oxford University Press.

Seffrin, P. M., Giordano, P. C., Manning, W. D., & Longmore, M. A. (2009). The influence of dating relationships on friendship networks, identity development, and delinquency. *Justice Quarterly*, *26*(2), 238–267.

Settersten, R. A. (2018). Nine ways that social relationship matter for the life course. In D. F. Alwin, D. H. Felmlee, & D. A. Kreager (Eds.), *Social networks and the life course: Integrating the development of human lives and social relational networks* (pp. 27–40). Springer International Publishing.

Settersten, R. A. Jr., & Ray, B. (2010). What's going on with young people today? The long and twisting path to adulthood. *The Future of Children, 20(1)*, 19–41.

Shanahan, M. J. (2000). Pathways to adulthood in changing societies: Variability and mechanisms in life course perspective. *Annual Review of Sociology*, *26*(1), 667–692.

Shanahan, M. J., Elder, G. H. Jr., Burchinal, M., & Conger, R. D. (1996). Adolescent earnings and relationships with parents: The work–family nexus in urban and rural ecologies. In J. T. Mortimer & M. D. Finch (Eds.), *Understanding families: Vol. 6. Adolescents, work, and family: An intergenerational developmental analysis* (pp. 97–128). Sage Publications, Inc.

Shanahan, M. J., Mortimer, J. T., & Johnson, M. K. (Eds.). (2016). *Handbook of the life course* (Vol. 2). Springer.

Shover, N. (1985). *Aging criminals.* Sage Publications.

Shover, N. (1996). *Great pretenders. Pursuits and careers of persistent thieves.* Westview Press.

Shulman, E. P., & Cauffman, E. (2011). Coping while incarcerated: A study of male juvenile offenders. *Journal of Research on Adolescence*, *21*(4), 818–826.

Shulman, S., & Connolly, J. (2013). The challenge of romantic relationships in emerging adulthood: Reconceptualization of the field. *Emerging Adulthood*, *1*(1), 27–39.

Shulman, S., & Connolly, J. (2016). The challenge of romantic relationship in emerging adulthood. In J. J. Arnett (Ed.), *The Oxford handbook of emerging adulthood* (pp. 230–244). Oxford University Press.

Siennick, S. E., & Widdowson, A. O. (2020). Juvenile arrest and later economic attainment: Strength and mechanisms of the relationship. *Journal of Quantitative Criminology, 38*, 23–50. https://link.springer.com/article/10.1007/s10940-020-09482-6

Steinberg, L. (2009). Adolescent development and juvenile justice. *Annual Review of Clinical Psychology, 5*, 459–485.

Steinberg, L., & Cauffman, E. (1996). Maturity of judgment in adolescence: Psychosocial factors in adolescent decision making. *Law and Human Behavior, 20*(3), 249–272.

Steinberg, L., & Schwartz, R. G. (2000). Developmental psychology goes to court. *Youth on Trial: A Developmental Perspective on Juvenile Justice, 1*, 9–10.

Stone, R. (2016). Desistance and identity repair: Redemption narratives as resistance to stigma. *British Journal of Criminology, 56*(5), 956–975.

Stone, R., & Rydberg, J. (2019). Parenthood, maturation, and desistance: Examining parenthood transition effects on maturation domains and subsequent reoffending. *Journal of Developmental and Life-Course Criminology, 5*, 387–414.

Strauss, A., & Corbin, J. (1998). *Basics of qualitative research techniques*. Sage Publications.

Subrahmanyam, K., Reich, S. M., Waechter, N., & Espinoza, G. (2008). Online and offline social networks: Use of social networking sites by emerging adults. *Journal of Applied Developmental Psychology, 29*(6), 420–433.

Sutherland, E. H. (1937). Review of Gluecks' later criminal careers. *Harvard Law Review*, 51: 184–186.

Syed, M., & Azmitia, M. (2010). Narrative and ethnic identity exploration: A longitudinal account of emerging adults' ethnicity-related experiences. *Developmental Psychology, 46*(1), 208.

Syed, M., & McLean, K. C. (2016). Understanding identity integration: Theoretical, methodological, and applied issues. *Journal of Adolescence, 47*, 109–118.

Tanner, J. L., & Arnett, J. J. (2009). The new life stage between adolescence and young adulthood. In A. Furlong (Ed.) *Handbook of youth and young adulthood: New perspectives and agendas* (pp. 39–45). Routledge.

Tanner, J. L., & Arnett, J. J. (2011). Presenting "emerging adulthood": What makes it developmentally distinctive. In J. J. Arnett, M. Kloep, L. B. Hendry, & J. L. Tanner (Eds). *Debating emerging adulthood: Stage or process* (pp. 13–30). Oxford University Press.

Taylor, S. J., Bogdan, R., & DeVault, M. (2015). *Introduction to qualitative research methods: A guidebook and resource*. John Wiley & Sons.

Thoits, P. A., & Virshup, L. K. (1997). Me's and we's. In R. D. Ashmore & L. Jussim (Eds.), *Self and identity: Fundamental issues* (pp. 106–133). Oxford University Press.

Thorne, A., McLean, K. C., & Lawrence, A. M. (2004). When remembering is not enough: Reflecting on self-defining memories in late adolescence. *Journal of Personality, 72*(3), 513–542.

Timmermans, S., & Tavory, I. (2012). Theory construction in qualitative research: From grounded theory to abductive analysis. *Sociological Theory, 30*(3), 167–186.

Uggen, C. (2000). Work as a turning point in the life course of criminals: A duration model of age, employment, and recidivism. *American Sociological Review, 65*(4), 529–546.

Uggen, C., & Janikula, J. (1999). Volunteerism and arrest in the transition to adulthood. *Social Forces*, *78*(1), 331–362.
Uggen, C., & Manza, J. (2005). Disenfranchisement and the civic reintegration of convicted felons. In C. Mele & T. A. Miller (Eds.), *Civil penalties, social consequences* (pp. 67–84). Routledge.
Uggen, C., Manza, J., & Behrens, A. (2004). 'Less than average citizen': Stigma, role transition, and the civic reintegration of convicted felons. In S. Maruna & R. Immarigeon (Eds.), *After crime and punishment: Pathways to offender reintegration* (pp. 258–290). Willan Publishing.
Uggen, C., & Massoglia, M. (2003). Desistance from crime and deviance as a turning point in the life course. In J. T. Mortimer & M. J. Shanahan (Eds.), *Handbook of the life course* (pp. 311–329). Springer.
Uggen, C., Vuolo, M., Lageson, S., Ruhland, E., & Whitman, H. (2014). The edge of stigma: An experimental audit of the effects of low-level criminal records on employment. *Criminology*, *52*(4), 627–654.
Uggen, C., & Wakefield, S. (2005). Young adults reentering the community from the criminal justice system: The challenge. In D. W. Osgood, E. M. Foster, C. Flanagan, & G. R. Ruth (Eds.), *On your own without a net: The transition to adulthood for vulnerable populations* (pp. 114–144). The University of Chicago Press.
Uggen, C., & Wakefield, S. (2008). What have we learned from longitudinal studies of work and crime? In A. M. Liberman (Ed.), *The long view of crime: A synthesis of longitudinal research* (pp. 191–219). Springer.
US Census Bureau Report Number C2KBR-24 and Press Release Number CB22-TPS.02.https://www.census.gov/library/publications/2003/dec/c2kbr-24.html#:~:text=Census%202000%20Brief%3A%20Educational%20Attainment%3A%202000,-August%202003&text=The%20education%20levels%20of%20the,high%2C%20according%20to%20Census%202000.&text=Of%20the%20182.2%20million%20people,at%20least%20a%20bachelor's%20degree. https://www.census.gov/newsroom/press-releases/2022/educational-attainment.html.
Van Maanen, J. (2011). *Tales of the field: On writing and ethnography*. University of Chicago Press.
Vaughan, B. (2007). The internal narrative of desistance. *The British Journal of Criminology*, *47*(3), 390–404.
Vespa, J. (2017). *The changing economics and demographics of young adulthood: 1975–2016* (pp. 1–23). US Department of Commerce, Economics and Statistics Administration, US Census Bureau.
Vignoles, V. L. (2018). Identity: Personal and social. In K. Deaux & M. Snyder (Eds.), *Oxford handbook of personality and social psychology, second edition*. Oxford University Press.
Vignoles, V. L., Schwartz, S. J., & Luyckx, K. (2011). Introduction: Toward an integrative view of identity. In S. J. Schwartz, K. Luyckx, & V. L. Vignoles (Eds.), *Handbook of identity theory and research* (pp. 1–27). Springer.
Visher, C. A., Winterfield, L., & Coggeshall, M. B. (2005). Ex-offender employment programs and recidivism: A meta-analysis. *Journal of Experimental Criminology*, *1*(3), 295–316. https://link.springer.com/article/10.1007/s11292-005-8127-x
Wakefield, S., & Apel, R. (2016). Criminal justice and the life course. In M. J. Shanahan, J. T. Mortimer, & M. K. Johnson (Eds.), *Handbook of the life course, volume II* (pp. 301–319). Springer International Publishing.

Wakefield, S., & Uggen, C. (2010). Incarceration and stratification. *Annual Review of Sociology*, *36*, 387–406.

Warner, C., & Remster, B. (2021). Criminal justice contact, residential independence, and returns to the parental home. *Journal of Marriage and Family*, *83*(2), 322–339.

Warr, M. (1998). Life-course transitions and desistance from crime. *Criminology*, *36*(2), 183–216.

Warr, M. (2002). *Companions in crime: The social aspects of criminal conduct*. Cambridge University Press.

Waterman, A. S. (1982). Identity development from adolescence to adulthood: An extension of theory and a review of research. *Developmental Psychology*, *18*(3), 341.

Western, B. (2002). The impact of incarceration on wage mobility and inequality. *American Sociological Review*, *67*, 526–546.

Western, B. (2006). *Punishment and inequality in America*. Russell Sage Foundation.

Wojciechowski, T. W. (2021). Snares or turning points? Examining the relevance of fatherhood entry timing and number of children for offending in adulthood. *Criminal Justice Review*, *46*(1), 5–19.

Wootton, B. (1962) *social science and social pathology*. Allen and Unwin.

Yamaguchi, K., & Kandel, D. B. (1985). On the resolution of role incompatibility: A life event history analysis of family roles and marijuana use. *American Journal of Sociology*, *90*(6), 1284–1325.

Yang, C. C., Holden, S. M., & Carter, M. D. (2017). Emerging adults' social media self-presentation and identity development at college transition: Mindfulness as a moderator. *Journal of Applied Developmental Psychology*, *52*, 212–221.

Zoutewelle-Terovan, M., Van Der Geest, V., Liefbroer, A., & Bijleveld, C. (2014). Criminality and family formation: Effects of marriage and parenthood on criminal behavior for men and women. *Crime & Delinquency*, *60*(8), 1209–1234.

INDEX

Note: Page numbers in **bold** refers tables and "n" refers notes.

For Product Safety Concerns and Information please contact our EU representative GPSR@taylorandfrancis.com
Taylor & Francis Verlag GmbH, Kaufingerstraße 24, 80331 München, Germany

www.ingramcontent.com/pod-product-compliance
Ingram Content Group UK Ltd.
Pitfield, Milton Keynes, MK11 3LW, UK
UKHW020000200926
475702UK00015B/2397
* 9 7 8 0 3 6 7 6 9 8 5 7 7 *